GOD

Still

ANSWERS

PRAYER

**OVER FIFTY MIRACULOUS STORIES
OF ANSWERS TO PRAYER**

Other Books by MARY WALLACE

GOD
Still
ANSWERS
PRAYER

OVER FIFTY MIRACULOUS STORIES

OF ANSWERS TO PRAYER

Compiled by Mary H. Wallace

WORD AFLAME PRESS

God Still Answers Prayer

by Mary H. Wallace

©2005, Word Aflame Press
    Hazelwood, MO 63042-2299

Cover Design by Simeon Young Jr.

Unless otherwise indicated, all quotations of Scripture are from The Holy Bible, King James Version.

Printed in United States of America

Printed by

WORD AFLAME PRESS
8855 Dunn Road, Hazelwood, MO 63042
www.pentecostalpublishing.com

Library of Congress Cataloging-in-Publication Data

Wallace, Mary H.
    God still answers prayer / Mary H. Wallace.
        p. cm.
    ISBN-13: 978-1-56722-648-5 (pbk.)
    ISBN-10: 1-56722-648-5 (pbk.)
  1.   Prayer--Christianity. I. Title.
    BV220.W35 2005
    248.3'2--dc22

                                                            2005009122

Contents

Dedication

I wish to dedicate this book to my beloved husband of more than sixty-two years, Rev. J. O. Wallace. I first met J. O. when he came with his father, Rev. J. W. Wallace, to minister in our small town of Finley, Tennessee. At fourteen, I was not too impressed, but when he came back the next year, I was very impressed. I was in Dyersburg High School and he was attending Draughan's Business College in Memphis.

We began to correspond. In 1941, after he finished college, he was inducted in the U. S. Army Medical Corps and shipped to California for training. We continued to write. In 1942 when I finished high school, he asked me to marry him.

God blessed us and called J. O. to the ministry. I found fulfillment as his helpmate. After the war was over and he was discharged from the army, he attended Bob Jones University then taught at the Pentecostal Bible

Institute in Tupelo, Mississippi. Then he pastored in Nashville, Oak Ridge and Knoxville, Tennessee. Later God used him especially in his business ability for over thirty-four years at the United Pentecostal Church World Evangelism Center as International Sunday School Director and also as the manager of the Pentecostal Publishing House. I worked alongside him teaching and writing Kindergarten and Nursery curriculum for Word Aflame Publications for twenty-three years and then served as editor for the Pentecostal Publishing House for over ten years.

My husband made me feel needed alongside his work. He especially encouraged me in writing. For over ten years, I had wanted to write a trilogy on Faith, Hope and Charity. We published the book, *Sow Seeds of Hope* in 2003, after he began to battle prostate cancer. Several times I noticed him reading that book.

We prayed earnestly and he fought a good fight, but on April 28, 2005, God took him home to be with Him. I must confess that my faith has been tried, but I still have hope. Most of all I know God gave us a wonderful life working for Him for over sixty-two years. I won't have any trouble writing about love, for I have known the love of a great man and our wonderful six children, not to mention God's abiding love. "Hitherto God has helped me," is one of my favorite scriptures. So goodbye for now, honey, and "I'll Meet You in the Morning Over There."

Foreword

My earliest memory of the names, J. O. and Mary Wallace, was when the Sunday school teacher handed me my first lesson sheet in class. Someone with the last name Wallace wrote most of our lessons. Sister Durham would reach up and gently pull the heavy bedsheet curtain across the strong wire to create our classroom. This was done to create classrooms in the one-room auditorium in the church. Each teacher would of necessity try to keep her voice down so not to distract the other classes. That was not always the case, so we tried to decide which teacher had the best story.

J. O. and Mary Wallace. Who were these people? Where did they live? What did they look like? Would I ever get to meet them in person? Someone who would write a lesson from the Bible and send it to my class for us to study the Bible was an important and very special person to a Sunday school student. My teacher shared her burden from the lessons that the Wallaces had written for her to use in her classroom.

Years later, I finally was privileged to meet the Wallaces. Since then I have sat in the front of several Sunday school classes and told the students, "I know the author of this lesson." As a missionary, I have taught their lessons and shared their books in many places in the continent of Africa over the past twenty-five years.

Now Mary Wallace has asked me to write the foreward to one of her books. I hope someone will take these true stories of the wonders of God and tell them far and wide. These true stories of miracles should be shared and never be allowed to die. When you read about these miracles, share them in testimonies, in family conversations, and you will be blessed and also challenged. Let the Lord use you to spread the good news.

Thank you, Sister Mary Wallace, for believing that it is important to write and share your beliefs so that everyone who will read one of these "Miracles" will be blessed and helped to believe God for a miracle of his own. Those will belong in the next book.

Jim Hall

1

My Testimony of Answered Prayer

by Annie Alford

How can I choose one answered prayer to write about from the innumerable blessings strewn through my life? In truth, my life itself is one long, long answered prayer.

Healings, miracles, deliverances, uplifting; these and many more are mine. Are there records of all these? Yes, written in heaven, engraved in my heart.

At sixteen, I even prayed for the love of the young man I later married. Afterward he often teased me, saying that since I talked to God about it, he had no choice in the matter. We had a long "happily ever after."

I prayed one prayer in my youth that I later questioned the wisdom of praying, yet God granted my request.

Vivid memories of healings for the eleven babies I dedicated to God before their birth bring waves of gratitude even now, when they are out of my care.

"Give us this day our daily bread" is not merely an example of prayer I read in the Bible. It is part of my life.

Many times I have received an answer immediately. Other times, I have prayed for years about a situation or a need before the answer came.

Certain kinds of prayers, scarcely mentioned, have added to the riches and happiness of my life. I will detail two of those. Perhaps they will add variety to the contents of this wonderful book that is destined to bless its readers.

Many years ago, in the 1940s, I learned the wealth of what I call "silent prayers." My husband was pastor of his first church. Times were hard. Money was scarce. One day I walked through the scantily furnished kitchen in the four-room parsonage thinking, "How wonderful it would be if we could but afford a can of peaches!" Later that same day, one of our neighbors came to share a few groceries with us; among them was a quart of home-canned peaches. Was this simply coincidence? You will never convince me!

This four-room house, my husband's first building project, with volunteer help, was our home. It was unfinished when we moved in. There were no kitchen cabinets. Above the sink, a window opened, revealing a scraggly yaupon. Every year a mockingbird built a nest in the yaupon and brightened my life with its varied notes of song.

One year a French Mocker drove the mockingbird away, leaving only the sassy cries of the blue jays in my neighbor's cornfield to enliven the world outside my window.

When the cold winter passed and birds began building nests, I looked longingly out my window, wishing my mockingbird would return. Suddenly she was there, singing her heart out, making my heart rejoice in the knowledge that God not only notes the sparrow but also the mockingbird and the secret desires of His children.

God's promise to us is that if we delight ourselves in Him, He will give us the desires of our heart.

These "desires" of our heart may be simple, or they may be extravagant. They are silent prayers, prayed in secret and rewarded openly.

Annie Alford

2

A Brother Brings Good News

by Dorothy Arthur

*I*t was a bright, cloudless morning in Hong Kong. The sun streamed through my bedroom window, filling me with a sense of thankfulness for how the Lord had blessed our missionary efforts in Hong Kong and Mainland China. Kneeling in prayer, I began to sincerely praise and worship the Lord, thanking Him for His many benefits.

Soon my praise turned into weeping as a pressing burden descended over me. The deep crushing feeling seemed to envelop my very being. It permeated my mind with a sense of doom. I felt a strong impression that my husband, Bob, was going to face death.

After travailing in the Spirit for some time, I felt some relief. However, several mornings that week, I experienced the same overwhelming feeling. Great sobbing and deep groaning swept over me as I repeated in prayer over and over, "Not my will, but Your will be done, Lord." I felt as though I was in a battle for my husband's life, but I also realized the importance of not fighting against God's will.

A month later we traveled to Taiwan to be with missionary Tommy Bracken in Kaohslung, Taiwan, for a speaking engagement. Kneeling at my seat before the service started, I found myself face-to-face with the same strong burden for my husband which I had been wrestling with for some time. It pounced on me, saturating my chest and stomach with an oppressive spirit, weighing me down as though a load of bricks were stacked on my chest. Loud sobs poured from my lips. I struggled in the Spirit for a release. I sincerely wanted to be liberated from this overpowering feeling, which was interrupting my life.

My husband walked over to me, laid his hands on my shoulder, and said, "Your will be done, Lord." I was amazed when I heard Bob quote the same words I had been articulating. He had no idea what I was earnestly praying about. I had never shared the awesome burden with him. Then I realized that the Spirit was speaking through him.

Returning to the United States some months later for deputation, we visited a church in Indiana. A brother approached Bob and asked if he could speak privately with him. It was a troubling message; there was danger facing Brother Arthur. This solemn announcement from a man of God, used in the gifts of the Spirit, placed a sobering heaviness on me. I no longer wanted to keep the burden, which I had been carrying for nearly six months, to myself, so I poured out my heart to Bob. "The reason you hear me weeping and moaning while praying in the morning is because of the seriousness of what I feel for your well-being." Bob blanched as the color drained from his features. A shadow of dismay crossed his face. He reeled under the sudden revelation of a death sentence being pronounced over him. Now he too was becoming an unwilling bearer of the heavy load which had invaded my life.

As we attended the Virginia United Pentecostal Church State Conference in Richmond, Virginia, our spirits were lifted by the spirited singing and anointed preaching, but nothing unusual happened. The burden continued to dog us. It was never far from our day-to-day business. It had become an unwelcome part of our lives. The spiritual conflict we faced had not been shared with anyone. We definitely believed the Lord would give us victory, and we continued to wait with great expectation. It happened on the last night of the conference. At the conclusion of the message, the preacher called for all the ministers to come to the front for special prayer. Temporarily I was stunned. My heart leaped in my chest, and a feeling of apprehension flowed over me as I noticed my husband stay frozen in his seat on the platform. It seemed as though he had suddenly become immobilized. In my mind, I was screaming, "Go to the altar! Go to the altar! Let the ministers pray for you. Surely God will do something tonight!" But he continued to sit with his head hanging down, like a man who had lost all hope.

Suddenly in the back of the congregation, a man sprang from his seat. Walking with purpose, he hurried to the platform with a look of destiny on his face. Making a quick leap onto the platform, he placed his hands on Bob's shoulders as he spoke words of life.

"Brother Arthur, the Lord just told me to tell you that everything is going to be okay." And everything has been all right since this prayer was answered in 1989.

19

3

A Revelation in a Prayer

by Erma Barley

One of the most wonderful privileges of living and working for God is the help He gives in everything, especially through prayer. Seemingly we can pray more earnestly if we know the details of a situation, but so many things happen in life that we cannot know all about them without God's help. Once while praying, Erma Barley, wife of pastor John Barley of Hobart, Indiana, experienced such a revelation.

I was praying one autumn Saturday morning in 2001, when suddenly I felt a burden for Christopher Strom, a thirteen-year-old boy in the church.

It seemed I could see him in a casket. I thought, "Oh, his grandparents lost a son. It would devastate them for Christopher to die." I begged God to spare his life.

Around noon that day, I saw an unknown truck in the church parking lot. Christopher was talking to the driver. They motioned toward our house. I didn't even think about my prayer. I just thought that perhaps Christopher had gotten into trouble with the man and was coming to the church for help. Soon Christopher and the man knocked at my door. They had an amazing story to tell:

Riding a bicycle, Christopher had entered a busy semi-rural highway at an angle and rode along the right-hand shoulder of the road. The man was driving his truck on the highway in the same direction. He saw the young boy and his bike, but traffic was coming the other way. He could not move toward the middle of the road.

His truck sideswiped the bicycle, breaking the front wheel and bringing it to a quick halt that dumped Christopher onto the roadside. Praise God, he was unhurt!

The truck driver put the battered bike into his truck and honored the youth's request to be taken to the church. I told Christopher of my prayer that morning. We praised God for His protection in that accident!

"I'm a Christian, too," said the truck driver. "I'm so thankful the boy was not hurt."

Can we not say that prayer protects us and prevents horrible things from happening?

Christopher Strom, age 13, escaped death.

4

The Miracle of the Drive Thru

by Margie Becton

Early afternoon on February 2, 2004, I saw my husband off to St. Louis from the Dallas area. Then I visited with an elderly lady of our church and went to the store and to the post office. As I drove down my driveway, I punched the garage door opener attached to the sun visor, heard and saw the door nearly opened to the top. At this point, I don't remember going in and through the garage and through the utility room, but I suddenly realized that I was in front of the fireplace in our living room. Quite astounding to drive through half of your house and not even know it!

The air bag did not release, so immediately I turned off the ignition. I could not open the car door (which was a blessing). No one was at home, so there was no need to scream or try to attract anyone's attention. When I saw a fallen door across my windshield along with Sheetrock falling and electrical wires hanging everywhere, I thought that I must have died. Temporarily I wished that I had.

I retrieved my cell phone from my purse and attempted to dial 911, but my phone would not work. We live in a low area for cell phones. I prayed then crawled to the back seat and held my phone up to the light of the back window. It worked! I got 911 and gave them my name, address, cell phone number, along with the numbers of my daughter, Renee Flowers, her husband, and the church. I also mentioned my age and circumstances, but I really had no clue as to what had happened.

Very soon the fire and police departments, ambulance, neighbors, and at last my family, who had been called, all arrived nearly at once.

What a miracle that I was not hurt, nor was anyone else hurt! My car was a wreck on the exterior, but no other car was involved. God was surely watching over me!

I was convinced that I needed to go to the nearest hospital emergency room but thought, "It will only be for a few hours." It turned out to be several days.

As I was being wheeled on the gurney to the ambulance, I heard my son-in-law, Rev. Rick Flowers, talking to my husband, Cleveland Becton, who had just arrived at the St. Louis airport. Brother Flowers told him that I had had a wreck but was not hurt, and that no one else was involved. I knew what the rest of the conversation would be, so I told the ambulance driver to hurry to get me to the hospital.

After learning all the facts, my husband immediately went to the airline counter and booked the very next flight back to Dallas. When he arrived in Dallas, he came straight to the hospital to see me.

We will ever be grateful to our grandsons, church members, and our home builder who came right away. Since the electrical wires were broken, the electricity needed to be cut off. Some temporary rewiring was done so that our freezer and other appliances could continue to operate.

David Starks, the one who built our house, put up temporary walls and made the house livable. This took quite a bit of adjusting, but we could continue to live at home. Our insurance adjusters arrived on the scene almost immediately.

A short time previously, we had walked our daughter, Renee, through our business papers in case something should happen to both her parents in one plight. She was able to give all the necessary information to both the auto and home insurance adjusters, which helped speed up all the necessary paperwork.

Before my husband arrived at the house, Robbie Fuller, Morris Starks, a block-away neighbor and also our church's music pastor, along with grandsons, Chase and Chad, Jonathan Fuller, and quite a few more, hauled away several truckloads of debris. A Rainbow vacuum was used to vacuum a lot of the Sheetrock dust, and the walls were built with temporary doors, etc. All damaged furniture and also the good pieces were taken to the garage.

In the hospital room, I wore a heart monitor day and night for four days. My pulse never got out of the forties. It was assumed that my pulse had gone down to the thirties, thus causing the blackout. After the following tests: CT head/brain scan w/o Co, chest IV, three EKGs, TEE with probe place, U/S carotid study DCO, Echo 2D & M-mode, Echo Doppler Complete, and an EEG, the doctors concluded that I needed a pacemaker.[1] I was told that I could not drive for six months. That was very depressing, but I had to face reality.

My regular cardiologist was out of town on a medical leave. Upon his return, his family had spring holidays. So several weeks passed before the pacemaker surgery was scheduled. After so many medical tests, they found no tumors and no strokes.

I felt good, so I decided to carry on with a speaking engagement with my daughter-in-law, Cheryl Becton, in the Corinth, Mississippi, area, driving from Nashville to Biggersville to speak for Sister Clenney's ladies' conference. We drove back to Nashville on Saturday afternoon, March 20, with Cheryl Becton doing the driving.

We had good services in Nashville on Sunday morning and were ready for church Sunday evening when another blackout occurred. I still can't figure out how I hit the back of my head and skinned my leg on the concrete garage floor from my knee to my ankle. There were several bad lacerations, so we rushed again to another emergency room, this time in St. Thomas Hospital, Nashville, Tennessee.

Again they found no tumor nor stroke, but they were very suspicious of a possible broken neck because of the terrible pain. After wearing a neck brace for five hours (except during different X-rays), I pled the blood and asked Jesus to please heal me and keep me from the famous halo-apparatus. God so graciously answered and honored my prayer. The head abrasions were very painful, causing puddles of blood and a very large swelling. Constant ice packing stopped the flow of blood. They also gave me another tetanus shot.

I insisted that I had not blacked out again. (I guess it would have added to the no-driving time). Apparently I had blacked out, as I did not call out for help nor say a word to Cheryl, who was just a few steps behind me. I don't know how many steps I fell, possibly three or four, but the concrete landing was not welcomed. Cheryl called to me, but I could not answer. She thought that I had fallen graveyard dead. She was very grateful when I came around shortly.

Two days later, I was back in Dallas. My head and leg stayed painful for quite a while—but painfully alive. This was another garage blackout miracle. No broken bones, no concussion, and no brain damage. My lacerated leg became infected and thus required two rounds of antibiotic infectious medicine. But again I was doing well.

To quickly conclude these miracles, on April 8, after several heart tests and heart catheterizing, I was given a pacemaker. I was doing wonderfully well. At last my pulse was regular, in the low seventies.

As one last miracle, my incision for the pacemaker did not heal and a terrible infection occurred. My cardiologist had never seen that kind of infection since his early medical college days. So he turned me over to an infectious care doctor and another doctor who was a surgeon. I had contracted staphylococcal infection in the hospital when they had put the pacemaker in.

Again there were many days of pain from the staph infection, and the doctors knew that the infection could go to the brain or to the heart and bloodstream. I was hospitalized for the third time in three months. But God fooled the experts and let the entire tests be negative. I had two gallium tests that would reveal if there was a spread of the infection, especially any that might have gone into my heart from the pacemaker. The staph infection had localized on the surface of the skin. This was my third miracle in such a short time.

My sister, Marilyn Miller, came twice to care for, encourage, and strengthen my faith during this whole ordeal. She even flew with me to speak at the Missouri ministers' wife retreat. She also stayed with me during the staph hospital infection. My dear sister stayed right there sharing my miracle.

I could never show enough gratitude toward my husband of fifty-seven years. For months he canceled most of his preaching engagements to be with me and to take care of all the endless paperwork, phone calls, doctor and hospital appointments, and all the insurance co-payments, etc. He did this all with tender loving care.

I Thessalonians 5:18 became my everyday motto: "In every thing give thanks: for this is the will of God in Christ Jesus concerning you." Paul said that we ought to give thanks always unto God.

I am enjoying my miracles. You can too, if you give thanks for everything.

Endnote

[1]CT scan 2 w/o Co—x-ray of body without use of intravenous contrast dye. EKG—echocardiogram, a procedure that uses sound waves to look at the structure and function of the heart. TEE—transesophageal echocardiogram, an EKG using a probe down the throat rather than an external device on the chest. U/S carotid study DCO—ultrasound view of the carotid artery, measuring Doppler cardiac output therein. Echo 2D & M-mode—EKG showing both two-dimensional (2D) and one-dimensional (M-mode) views. Echo Doppler Complete—EKG that measures speed and direction of the heart's blood flow. EEG—electroencephalogram, a procedure that detects, traces, and records brain wave activity.

Miraculously, the air bag did not release.

Only the bumper remained in the garage.

A door, sheetrock, and electrical wires fell all around the car.

The car stopped right
at the fireplace.

Sister Becton's car parked
in her living room.

5

A Search for Something More

by Aaron Bockman
(as told to Tobi Bockman)

When I was five, my family moved to St. Louis and began attending a small, non-denominational church. In a child's trusting heart, a belief in Jesus existed. I loved the worship service and children's church. I was so into the Bible stories that I felt sorry for Judas and tried hanging myself.

Surviving that escapade, we remained in this church until I was a seventh grader. I remember a confrontation between my parents and the pastor where tears were shed, and the family changed churches—this time to a much larger congregation. Two years later, the family quit going to church altogether.

As the transition between churches was occurring, I started hanging out with Adam. The son of an alcoholic, Adam was cool. He drank, smoked, and led a not so pure life. I wanted to be just like him, so, at the age of fourteen, I started down the road of impurity. When I was fifteen, I began drinking. Knowing I couldn't purchase my own alcohol, I stole a bottle of Jagermiester from a local grocery store. And so began my journey away from a God I'd learned about in Sunday school.

Remembering what I had been taught, I knew my actions were wrong. Still, it was fun and made me feel good. The first night I got drunk, I was at a girl's house with my friend Caleb, playing poker with Caleb and two girls. The girl's father had a bar. I filled half of a glass with Coca-Cola and the other half with Bourbon. This became a ritual. It was free alcohol—free fun. When I couldn't obtain it any other way, I would steal it.

Alcohol and promiscuity were not the only things in which I dabbled. Starting an expensive habit at fifteen, I tried my first joint. When I couldn't get it from my brother, I would use the money I made bathing dogs. An adventurous sort, I tried huffing gasoline, crack cocaine, and a few other drugs.

Realizing that their children were beyond their help, my parents forced my brother and me to join a drug treatment program called United Behavioral Systems. Taught by people with PhDs, the program didn't relate to us on an equal level. However, the program required that its participants choose a twelve-step program and attend a few of that program's meetings. I chose Crossroads, a twelve-step program for young people. (The twelve-step program encourages you to admit that you have a problem and that only God or a higher power can help you. You are also urged to clean up your past, grow a deeper relationship with your chosen higher power, and help someone else do the same thing.)

At my first Crossroads meeting, I met my best friend Brandon. Brandon, a former heroin addict and three years older, was chosen as my sponsor—the twelve-step-teacher. During this initial meeting, Brandon gave me the rules of the program. After the rules, Brandon and I discovered a shared love for hockey.

During my first six months into Crossroads, I drank a few more times and huffed rubber cement and gasoline. While I finally broke the drug and alcohol addiction, I couldn't stop my promiscuous life style. It became my drug of choice. On St. Patrick's Day of 1997, a friend invited me to a party where alcohol and women were present. I went for the women. Here I found a blonde without a name, but drunk and willing. After I had seduced her, I remembered feeling so horrible that I felt no emotion. When the numbness settled in, I decided that since I felt nothing, I could drink. As I put the glass up to my lips, my friend yelled, "Don't let him drink! He's eighteen months sober!" I was then made to leave the party.

After that party, I began to realize that my impure actions were taking the place of the alcohol and drugs. I told myself I would practice abstinence until I was in love. Three months later, I began "working the steps" and started feeling good about myself, but deep inside, I knew something was missing. My life and friends became Crossroads. Crossroads was a place where you could party without getting drunk, be loud without getting drunk, and be crazy without getting drunk. However, everyone in Crossroads, it seemed, smoked. Having never picked up the habit before, I started smoking to join in with my new "family." I also moved into a house with several Crossroaders.

While this program encouraged me to stop my addictions, it changed my conception of God. I began praying to the concept of love—praying to a general god. I would pray every morning and every night to this god with no name and no face. In March of 1998, my brother, who had been in jail for a while, was released. During his time in a cell, my brother had read the entire Bible through. When he moved in with me, he told me that he had been reading the Bible and that he had turned back toward God. So filled with conviction, I remember shaking as my brother witnessed to me.

After this, I began reading my Bible again and praying to the God of the Bible. One day, while working at Subway, I was cleaning out a bread oven, all the while complaining to God that I was never going to get a girlfriend. An audible voice assured me, "Aaron, I'm going to take care of you." Thinking that God was going to supply me with a girlfriend, I told my brother of my experience. My brother informed me that God didn't just mean a girlfriend that God would take care of everything in my life. After attending several churches, searching for the truth, I settled on a local, non-denominational church.

In May of 1999, I graduated from Crossroads and began going to Alcoholics Anonymous (AA) meetings. Trying to make something of myself, I started college and went for nine consecutive months. During this time, I delivered pizzas and served as valet and busboy at a fine-dining restaurant. One night, a lady came into the restaurant and told me of this wonderful job opportunity where I could get on-the-job training and not have a degree. I went in for an interview at John Hancock Financial Services and was hired. Beginning my new career in the insurance business, I had to make a set amount of commission before being put on contract. Discarding the fine-dining job, I worked for John Hancock during the day and delivered pizzas at night.

While delivering pizzas, I worked with a girl named Ellen. She was young and fun. We dated on and off for a little over a year. I had now promised myself that I was going to remain abstinent until I was married. Still, Ellen and I would mess around. Knowing I was sinning, I would pray and repent every night and ask God why I couldn't live right. I did everything I knew to do. I went to church regularly, paid tithes, prayed, and read the Bible. Why was I still cussing, smoking, telling dirty jokes, and messing around with girls?

In August of 2000, Natalie Black[1] came to work at John Hancock as an assistant to two of my co-workers. She was cool, but quiet. Something was special about her. At first we didn't speak much besides the occasional "hello." At one point, I asked her if she was a Christian. She confirmed that she was, and I had found myself a friend. From that time, we would often discuss Christian music.

One evening, Natalie, another man, and I were all working late in the office. I had the sudden urge to tell her my story. I thought she might be able to provide an answer as to why I was still sinning and why I felt so empty. After listening, Natalie asked me if I had received the Holy Ghost like the people in the Book of Acts. I knew that I had because I thought that I'd spoken in tongues. She then asked how I felt when I spoke in tongues. I told her I didn't feel any different. She explained that the indwelling of the Holy Ghost helps a person to understand what's right and wrong and aids in resisting temptation. She invited me to come to church with her. I told her I would, but inwardly I was thinking, "You don't get it! Changing churches won't solve the problem." I ended up oversleeping instead of attending.

A week or so later, I began rethinking my answer—did I have the Holy Ghost like Natalie had described? Could I speak in tongues? Driving around in my car, I decided to see if I had the gift of tongues. I started speaking gibberish, and when "Yabba-dabba-do!" came out of my mouth, I decided that maybe I didn't have what Natalie had.

While Natalie was trying to show me the truth, I was still seeing Ellen. A friend had given me a condom on a key chain. It was too much temptation, and the promise I had made to myself went out the window. After this girl had left my apartment, I sat alone—ashamed, destroyed. I had taken advantage of a girl I didn't love. Each time I would cross the line, I would ask God to forgive me. This is the last straw, I thought, God's not going to forgive me this time. The telephone rang. It was Natalie.

"Hey, Aaron! You want to come to church with me?"

"What could it hurt?" I told myself.

When I walked into the church, the first thing I recalled was the smiling faces. These people were happy! After the Gateway College of Evangelism chorale sang, a preacher got up to preach. He was a big man who yelled when he got excited. I noticed that these people liked to stand up and sit down a lot. They were crazy people, but they had something I didn't have.

When the altar call was made, Natalie asked me if I wanted the Holy Ghost. Without hesitation, I went to the front left corner of the church where I was met by Kyle Flowers.[2] Kyle told me all I needed to do was repent of my sins and start praising God. I began spouting off all my sins and telling God I was sorry. I didn't care if the on-lookers were getting an earful! After I was through, Kyle told me that the highest praise I could give God was hallelujah. With both hands in the air, I began shouting the highest praise. On the second hallelujah, I saw a ball of light come from above and hit me in the forehead. As the ball of light went through me, I thought, "This is it! This is what I've been missing." Then I began to speak in tongues as the Spirit gave the utterance! That night, November 19, 2000, I was baptized by immersion in Jesus' name as Jesus washed away all my sins (Acts 2:38).

Just two weeks after receiving the baptism of the Holy Spirit, I quit smoking—cold turkey.

I will tell you that since finding the truth and receiving the Holy Ghost, life hasn't been perfect, but I have peace, power over temptations, and unspeakable joy.

(Aaron and his beautiful, Pentecostal bride, Tobi, attend Apostolic Pentecostal Church in St. Louis, Missouri, pastored by Stephen Willeford. Aaron enjoys being a Sunday school teacher for the fourth and fifth grade boys and willingly shares his testimony to anyone who will lend him an ear.)

(Editor's Note: All names have been changed except those noted.)

Endnotes

[1-2]The names of Natalie Black and Kyle Flowers have not been changed.

Aaron before

Aaron and Tobi

6

Miracle on the George Washington Bridge

by Pauline Brash

Wisdom is better than strength (Ecclesiastes 9:16).

October 1990

Our daughter, Charmaine, and her baby girl Veronica had come to visit with us for a while. Her husband John had returned to Pittsburgh and decided that on this particular night, he would meet us halfway to get his family.

The arrangements seemed workable. Henry (my husband) became uneasy a little while later and suggested that maybe we should have him come back to New York and rest overnight. "Since they have the baby," he said, "it will be wiser to travel in the daytime."

Since he was outvoted, we got in the car, prayed for protection, and drove her to the meeting spot, just across the George Washington Bridge. We got there safely in spite of the fact that we did not have a car seat for the baby and our daughter did not wear her seat belt. We felt no fear nor anticipated any dreadful thing happening.

We said our good-byes and began our journey home. Henry was tired so I drove. Just about halfway across the bridge, there was construction. Most of the equipment and work vehicles were parked in the far right lane. I decided to drive in the far left lane. My husband began to doze. Everything seemed okay, until . . .

I saw a flash of light in the right side mirror, which I discovered were headlights from another car that was just too close to our car. Simultaneously, I heard a click and felt the car jerk. All the foot pedals began to be controlled by some other force as the car began to slide uncontrollably on its side and all four wheels began to hit the divider from the other highway. It felt like someone had taken a hold on the car and was determined to push it over the side of the divider into oncoming traffic.

I let go of the steering wheel, closed my eyes, and prayed silently. It happened so unexpectedly and took me completely by surprise. Henry awoke and I heard him shout the name Jesus. For just a little while, it seemed like the car settled down. Then that force started again to hit the car against the wall. Henry shouted, "Jesus," the second time, and amazingly, the car settled down as though the fingers that were clutching it could not hold it any longer. It bounded across the street to the right and just rested against the opposite wall. We were still intact with our seat belts around us. A song of thanksgiving began to play on the car stereo system, "Thank You, Lord, for another day!"

The cause of the accident was a twenty-year-old drunken female miscalculating the space for her car to overtake me on the right. When her car collided with ours, it got out of control and crashed into the wall on the right.

The two young ladies suffered serious injuries. It didn't appear that they were wearing their seat belts. One suffered a fractured skull and the other lost some teeth when her mouth hit the dashboard. Blood was everywhere.

We stayed with them until the paramedics and the police came. We then took a good look at the entire scene before us. People seemed to be everywhere. What caught my attention was that on this four-lane highway, the traffic had stopped and was being blocked by the big semis that were traveling behind us. And then it dawned on us that a great event had just taken place and we had played a major role in it.

Henry and I were able to walk away from our car without a scratch. Of course, a day or so after, we found out what whiplash felt like. But we rejoiced as we gave our testimony on Sunday. This was a notable miracle!

1. If the accident had taken place before we left our daughter and granddaughter with our son-in-law, the outcome could have been quite worse.

2. The Lord allowed the accident to happen to show us that He's still in control and in His hands, there's only safety and nothing can touch us there except Him!

7

God Changes Things

by Paul Daniel Buford

A Testimony of God's Healing Power

On January 15, 1996, I first noticed an odd feeling in my stomach area. It was not a pain but just a "different" feeling. I was joining with our church, Florissant Valley Apostolic Church, on a three-day fast, at the time and thought that I was just hungry. On the second day of the fast, the feeling was more intense—not a pain but I just felt different. I ate a little bit of soup at the end of second day, thinking the feeling would go away, but it did not. I fasted the third day, and the feeling persisted. Again, I ate some soup at the close of the day, but the feeling did not go away.

That night I noticed my eyes and skin were yellow. The following day I showed my jaundiced condition to my wife, and we made an appointment with our doctor for the next day. After about a week of blood tests, various scans, and an endoscopic procedure, the doctors discovered a blockage in my lower bile duct. This blockage prevented the normal flow of bile, which backed up into my liver, causing the jaundiced condition.

The doctor came to our hospital room on the evening of Wednesday, January 24, and discussed the situation with us. He felt that surgery was required to remove the blockage, but a surgeon would be coming in on Thursday to discuss further our options. The surgeon came and really offered only one option—the Whipple Procedure. This would involve removing the tumor, the lower bile duct, a portion of the upper bile duct, one-fourth of the stomach, the "head and neck" of the pancreas, the duodenum, and the gallbladder. Then the small intestines would be lifted up and connected to the remaining portions of the upper bile duct, stomach, and pancreas. This procedure was the only viable option for two reasons: first, the blockage had to be removed and the bile duct reconnected, with this procedure being the best way to reconnect, and second, in the case of any malignancy, the parts of the body that adjoined the offending tumor would be totally removed. Since in most cases a tumor in this area was malignant and would not respond to chemotherapy or radiation, total removal was the best option. The surgeon felt that the surgery needed to be done within twenty-four to forty-eight hours lest the liver be damaged as well.

After much prayer and godly counsel, and having a second surgeon review my files and give the same opinion, we decided to have the surgery done. It was scheduled for the next day. People were praying for me around the world, thanks to a network of family, friends, and churches. Words of encouragement and effectual, fervent prayers came from ministers, saints, family, and even the hospital staff.

During the surgery on Friday, January 26, 1996, a host of people gathered with my wife and family to hold them up before God. Their support meant so much at that particular time. During the surgery, the surgeon sent word that he had removed the tumor, sent it to pathology, and was continuing with the Whipple Procedure. Following the surgery, he came out to speak with my wife. She invited the group with her to hear the report as well. The surgeon said that he had removed the tumor and, according to the pathology work done on it during the surgery, it was malignant. He told us that an oncologist would be meeting with us soon.

After spending several days in intensive care and then in a private room, we still had not heard from the oncologist. My wife questioned the surgeon about this, and he said that the doctors were holding off for the present. Several more days passed, and we asked the question again. The surgeon said that he was beginning to see a glimmer of hope; the tissues surrounding the bile duct were not contaminated. We rejoiced and thanked God for that report. The surgeon said that "Somebody" upstairs was listening!

As the days passed and we did not hear any further reports, we grew anxious. The doctors finally told us that they were sending the slides and work to another hospital so that more pathology work could be done. Finally the day came when the doctors told us the results. The pathology work done on the tumor during the surgery showed that it was definitely malignant. However, the tests done later in the hospital on the original tumor as well as the various parts removed showed no malignancy at all. Because of the conflict in the hospital's two reports, they sent everything off to another hospital for a complete reevaluation. The report came back again, absolutely no malignancy! The doctors had no explanation for this change except that "Somebody" upstairs was listening!

I do not understand the manner in which God works, but I do know that He does work! I am nothing special, and I am not good, but I am extremely grateful for the healing touch that God has given to me. There was a recovery time following the surgery, but thanks be to Jesus Christ, I have a clean bill of health nine years later—absolutely no malignancy! God changes things!

Paul Daniel Buford

8

Resurrection Sunday

by Ralph Buie

When a Daisy Bloomed Again

It started out as a very typical New York City Sunday morning in April 1996. Mayor Rudy Giuliani was continuing his two-year campaign against city crime with time left over to clean up Times Square and make it presentable. British Labor Party leader Tony Blair was in town visiting United Nations officials on the East Side while former Polish President Lech Walesa toured southern Connecticut. Even the Cunard Line's *Queen Elizabeth* had docked on the lower West Side two days earlier after a ninety-five-day round-the-world tour. But in spite of all this, the only truly memorable event of the day for the congregation of the United Pentecostal Church of Greater New York would be the spectacular resurrection of Daisy Veronica Bonello.

Since 1937, the church had been located on the Upper West Side, housed in an eighteen-foot-wide, classic brownstone building. "The Ninety-Second Street

Church," as everyone called it, had held services there for almost sixty years. The sanctuary was about fifty-five feet long with an interior width of sixteen feet. It was a unique sanctuary to say the least. In spite of these limitations, the church family had learned to worship God there with genuine liberty. And worship they did! The congregation was known for its energetic praise, and this Sunday would be no different.

From the moment the assistant pastor, Robert Linder, opened the service, the Holy Ghost was present. The service was unusually anointed and everyone sang enthusiastically and praised God with a fresh zeal. The congregation only paused reluctantly from worship when Linda Canton welcomed the first-time visitors, but the praise erupted again when the congregation finished welcoming the guests by clapping. As with most Pentecostal services, magnifying Jesus was the first priority while offerings or announcements played an important but secondary role. The Spirit of God was still powerfully evident as Sorle Diih, the missions director, came to the pulpit to give his missions report.

Daisy Bonello was sitting about halfway back on the right side of the sanctuary. She was a faithful saint and had served God from her youth back in Jamaica. On this particular Sunday, she was singing joyfully every song from memory. She never had to refer to the hymnbook for help. Even at eighty-two years of age, this small lady loved to sing and pray and lift up the name of Jesus. It seemed a natural talent. It wasn't something she practiced. It was simply a part of her. She loved the Lord and gave Him her very best in every service. Then came the missions report. That meant she would have to remain politely quiet until Brother Diih was finished.

Brother Diih, a Nigerian emigrant, speaking with a heavy West African accent, was eagerly reporting the number of souls that had received the baptism of the Holy Ghost on the foreign field when Sister Daisy slowly slumped to the right in her pew. It seemed to happen in slow motion. At first, no one really noticed, but then, her glasses fell into the aisle followed by her dentures. Pearl Wilson was sitting behind Daisy on the opposite side of the sanctuary and had seen the glasses and dentures fall. For some unexplained reason, Daisy was not making any effort to retrieve them. Confused, Pearl wanted to get the attention of Josephine Bonello, Daisy's daughter, who was sitting three pews ahead. Josephine was a registered nurse at nearby St. Luke's Hospital. She'd know what to do.

"Josephine! Josephine!" Pearl tried to whisper, but it came out louder than a whisper. Since Brother Diih was speaking also, Josephine didn't respond at first. "Josephine!" Pearl said much louder the second time. "Look at your mother!" Josephine turned toward the voice; then she saw her mother slumped motionless in the pew. Rushing from her seat, she reached her mother and tried to determine the problem. Lenora Olique, who had been sitting next to Daisy, jumped out of the pew to give Josephine more room to help her mother. Lenora started praying in the aisle, and at that moment, time seemed to stop for Josephine.

At times like this, reality can be cruel. Josephine felt for a pulse . . . first, at the wrist . . . nothing . . . then, at the neck . . . again, nothing, not even a weak pulse. Placing her hand on her mother's chest, she hoped and prayed for some sign of respiration. Nothing . . . not the slightest movement . . . nothing! She placed her hand near her mother's mouth . . . and prayed again, hoping to feel breath . . . no, none . . . nothing! Desperate, she bent low so that her face was just an inch from her mother's mouth . . . another quick prayer . . . nothing. All the signs were bad.

As a medical professional, Josephine had seen this all too often before. She understood what all this meant. She couldn't fool herself or deny the facts . . . no pulse . . . no respiration . . . nothing, and that equaled no life. No doubt about it, Josephine felt herself yielding to the inevitable. Her mother was dead! "Well," a strange voice said to no one in particular, "she's lived a long and blessed life. And she was a child of God . . . faithful and true. Why don't you just let her go?" Josephine was shocked. It was her own voice! "Wait a minute . . . I said, wait! There's one last thing! Clear the airway!" She laid her mother on the pew and gently pulled her head back, depressed her tongue, and opened her mouth. But nothing really changed. "How much time has passed? How long have I been doing this? When is enough, enough?" she wondered.

But as Josephine struggled in the pew with her mother's limp body, the church family had reacted immediately. Someone was sent to the church office to call 911 while everyone else fell on their knees and began to pray with purpose and power. No one remained indifferent or unfeeling. Everyone found a place to pray and everyone called upon the one, healing name—Jesus! Some cried out aloud. Some quietly interceded. Some wept and prayed and some spoke with other tongues. Others prayed in groanings that could not be uttered. Daisy may have been dead, but heaven was being bombarded with a constant stream of focused prayer and intercession that was declaring war on death, hell, and the grave. Death would not take Daisy without a fight! Later, no one could remember how much time had passed. Maybe twenty minutes or so. But as the seconds ticked by, time was the real enemy.

Josephine felt her heart sinking as nothing she tried seemed to make any difference. Desperate and frustrated, she looked around the sanctuary for help or encouragement. Everybody was praying . . . behind her . . . in the aisle . . . at the altar. All were calling on Jesus. Then she heard someone boldly speaking with other tongues. But the sound was so close! Josephine turned in the pew to see her mother praising and magnifying the Lord in a heavenly language! Before Josephine could really comprehend what this meant, Sister Daisy sat up in the pew! Moments before, she was clinically dead! For over twenty minutes, there were absolutely no signs of life . . . nothing. But now, Daisy was sitting up in the pew giving God thanksgiving for His mercy and grace! There was no denying it, Daisy was alive again.

A roar of celebration went up. The church family had realized that Daisy was sitting up and rejoicing in other tongues. People were laughing and crying at the same time, hugging one another and smiling from ear to ear. No one knew exactly how it had happened, but everyone knew what had happened! Sister Daisy was dead, and now, she was clearly alive. Prayer had been made. Heaven was attentive. And angels had been dispatched with an answer. God had miraculously raised Sister Daisy from the dead . . . right there in the pew! It was the Sunday when a Daisy bloomed again. The rejoicing continued as the emergency medical service team entered the back of the building, looking for their patient. But the hand of God had already done the necessary work. Daisy had just experienced her very own Resurrection Sunday!

Daisy couldn't understand why the medical team wanted her to put on an oxygen mask and lay down on their stretcher. "After all," she said, "I don't feel bad enough to go to the hospital." But after some explanation of what had transpired, Daisy agreed to be taken to St. Luke's Hospital just across town. In the emergency room, her vital signs were all stable, and she was admitted for observation. The next day, surgeons implanted a pace-maker to regulate her slower than normal heartbeat. She was released after two days.

Epilogue

It was my privilege to pastor Sister Daisy Bonello for many years. She was a sweet lady and a precious saint who loved the Lord with all her heart. After her personal miracle in 1996, Daisy continued to serve the Lord and faithfully attend church with an increased determination for the next seven years. In late 2003, she suffered a debilitating stroke, and she required constant medical attention. Sister Daisy's ninetieth birthday was October 28, 2004. Two days later, a very special birthday party was held in her honor at the Amsterdam House, her residence for almost a year. At that birthday party, I was honored to hug Sister Daisy's neck, kiss her cheek, and tell her I loved and appreciated her. Five days after her ninetieth birthday, Sister Daisy was quietly promoted from this life into His everlasting presence.

Sister Daisy Bonello

Sister Daisy Bonello

9

God Pays His Debts and Keeps His Word

by Marilyn Chennault

I had worked at the church office all day, then hurried home to cook dinner for my husband, Brother Nallen W. Chennault. Every time I had called that day, he didn't seem to feel well. He had a bad infection in his foot. This is always a serious matter as he is diabetic. After dinner I needed to go to the church to play the piano for youth services.

When I returned home, he wasn't in his chair, so I began to look for him. I called and he answered me from the bathroom. As I entered the room, he was standing facing the wall, in total confusion. He told me that he could not find his way out. I led him to the hallway, where he collapsed. I ran next door for help to put him in the car so we could take him to the emergency room at the hospital.

He was in a semi-coma. His temperature was 103 degrees, and with each passing hour, it raised a degree. They packed him in ice that brought the fever down for a while, but this pattern continued as he had edema, which reached to his groin, in that foot and leg.

The church and the ministers of the district offered much prayer. But he did not seem to be getting any better. On the third day while I sat by his bed, they packed him once again in ice to bring his fever down. His doctor told a friend of ours that he would not make it.

I knew that I needed to touch the Lord on my husband's behalf. I got down on the floor behind his bed and began to pray. I told the Lord that I knew all the Scripture verses and all things that could be said in this situation because I had quoted them to other people. But now I needed something different to know that He had really spoken to me. About an hour or so later, the Lord spoke and said, "He that hath pity upon the poor lendeth unto the LORD; and that which he hath given will he pay him again" (Proverbs 19:17).

I got up from prayer and sat in the chair very upset because I did not know what this scripture had to do with this situation. While I sat there, the Lord began to talk to me, reminding me of the hundreds of people that Brother Chennault had helped over the forty-plus years we had been here. I-35 passes through our city. We have received many calls from evangelists, missionaries, and other people who were broke down or needed money to continue their journey, a place to stay, or food to eat. Also Brother Chennault has helped many people in our own city and congregation with food and finances.

There is no way that God owes us anything except when we have pity and give to the poor; then God always pays His debts. I began to rejoice and thank the Lord that He was going to reward my husband in remembrance of that scripture.

About that time, Brother Chennault turned over in bed and called my name. It had been three days since he had called my name. I went to his bedside and he said, "Marilyn, did you see Him?"

"Who?" I asked.

"Jesus," he said.

"No," I replied.

Then he said, "Jesus asked me if I wanted to go home with Him or not. I said that I would like to stay here a little longer with you."

I began to weep because I knew that God had heard and answered prayer.

From that time on, my husband began to get better. In just a day or two, we went home. God is a never failing God, and He always keeps His Word.

Bro. Chennault

57

Bro. and Sis. Chennault

10

The Miracle of
My Conversion

by Wayne Chester

asketball was the most important thing in my life. I had been very successful in my college career as a basketball player, having played four years for Bethel College of McKenzie, Tennessee. I served as the captain of the team for two years and made the all-conference team my senior year in college. I also was selected in the Who's Who in American Colleges and Universities my senior year.

I was not married when I first started coaching basketball; therefore, all my free time was spent with something that had to do with basketball. I started my coaching career at Bell City High School in Bell City, Missouri. Central High School in Camden, Tennessee, contacted me and asked me to come to Camden to be the athletic director and basketball coach. I had a very successful tenure as basketball coach at Central High School in Camden, Tennessee. One of the years, we won thirty-six games and only lost three if I remember correctly. I had an outstanding basketball player by the name of

Danny Boyd, who now is a Pentecostal preacher. Danny scored 104 points in one basketball game. He still holds the state record for the most points scored in one game.

But he became an important part in the story of my conversion, as his mother was a Pentecostal lady. I often had to drive Danny home from basketball practice and therefore became closely associated with his family.

His mother was continually inviting me to attend Sunday school at the Rushings Chapel Pentecostal Church. I attended with Danny occasionally, even though I had been a member of Missionary Grove Baptist Church since I was twelve years old.

Rev. Jimmy Mead, a young evangelist, preached a revival at Rushings Chapel, and I began to attend the services.

God convicted me of my sins. I made my way to the altar in that little country church. It seemed I wept a bucket of tears. They took me down to the Tennessee River and baptized me in Jesus' name. I had been baptized there when I was twelve years old but not in the name of Jesus!

I began to seek for the Holy Ghost. I wanted it more than anything else in the world. One night we kept the saints at the church until 2:00 A.M., seeking the Lord. We sought out churches that were having services, in order to go and seek the Lord. I was filled with the Holy Ghost on a Sunday night at the Camden First United Pentecostal Church.

I was still coaching basketball at this time. I finished out my year and then resigned as basketball coach. I didn't know what I was going to do as far as a vocation. I went to Nashville and worked for a few weeks and then decided that I would go to Stockton, California, and attend the Western Apostolic Bible College. While there I taught in the high school department and then attended as many classes as I possibly could in the Bible school, trying to hide the Word of God in my heart.

During this time, God called me to preach the gospel.

At the Christmas break, I went back to Tennessee and married Carolyn Sue Wright.

During my Christian life, God has had His hand on my life and has blessed me in so many ways. One particular thing comes to mind. I was assistant principal at Central High School in Camden, Tennessee, and was also pastoring the First United Pentecostal Church. Then I was selected by the Tennessee District of the United Pentecostal Church to serve as district secretary after Brother M. H. Hansford had retired from that position.

I had just built a new house in Camden. At that time, the interest rate was about 17 percent, therefore, I was wondering if I would be able to sell the house as the district board was requiring that I move to Jackson. Real estate was at a standstill. However, God moved on the scene and sent me a buyer for my house. I was able to sell it to the first person who looked at it.

Later God saw fit to allow me to be elected district superintendent of the Tennessee District after Brother L. H. Benson's retirement.

God has brought me a long, long way from where I used to be. I will be eternally grateful for His love and mercy that He has bestowed on me.

I am retiring from the superintendent's position in April 2005, and I know that God will continue to be with me during my golden years of retirement.

Wayne Chester, basketball coach.

Wayne Chester during coaching days.

Danny Boyd, third from right.

Boyd's Big Scoring Splurge Suggested By His Buddies

By GENE PEARCE
TENNESSEAN Sports Writer

CAMDEN, Tenn. — Camden's basketball team committed premeditated scoring mayhem Friday.

"Everybody on the team said they wanted me to set a record," Danny Boyd, a bushy eyed sharpshooter, said yesterday after eclipsing every known Tennessee scoring record in a resounding 130-43 win at Clarksburg Friday.

BOYD, a senior who stands 5-11 and weighs 155 pounds, scored 104 points, although he didn't play the final four minutes of the game.

"Coach (Wayne Chester) said it was up to the team about my trying to set a scoring record," a shy Boyd said. "Jimmy Johnson and James Bell (teammates) suggested it to the coach and he said it was okay if everybody agreed."

Boyd did his best, but it took plenty of urging from teammates, and even a fan from the opposing Clarksburg crowd, to push the honor student to his record mark.

DANNY, who has a 95 scholastic average and who is a member of the Beta Club, scored 55 points in the first half as the Lions piled up a team total of 65 against Clarksburg, which was taking its third defeat from powerful Camden.

"I was embarrassed about scoring all those points, but everybody kept telling me to keep going," Boyd said. "I didn't want to play the last half.

"The way I was hitting that jump shot was fantastic," he added. "The best I can remember I only made eight or 10 crips. The rest were jump shots."

Danny, just 16 years old, hit 44 field goals and 16 free throws.

Here's his scoring by periods:

	FG	FT	Total
First	11	2	24
Second	11	9	31
Third	13	1	27
Fourth	9	4	22
Total	44	16	104

"Our shot charts are incomplete, but I know for sure he hit well over 50 per cent from the field," Chester said.

WITH ABOUT four minutes remaining in the game (high schools play eight-minute quarters), Chester took Boyd out with 100 points to his credit.

"He was tired and I thought he had enough, but some Clarksburg fan came over and said let him score 104 to break Janet Hays' record of 103," Chester said.

Janet Hays scored 100 points for Henry against Puryear during the 1955-56 season. Apparently the Clarksburg fan had been misled about Hays' total.

Boyd's goal had been the 80-point record set by Gordon Taylor of Trezevant during the 1953-54 season, also against Puryear.

BOYD NOW has 510 points for the season for an average of 26.9 a game. However, he is a long way from the State scoring lead. Rutledge's A. W. Davis has scored 713 points in 20 games for an average of 35.1. Davis is expected to break the longstanding record of Bailey Howell, the former Middleton player who scored 1,186 points.

Danny's average could be a lot better," Chester said. "But we haven't had much trouble in a lot of our games and he's only played a half in many of them." The Lions are 18-1.

Chester was surprised to find out that his club had not set a team record. Loudon is the holder of that honor, having beaten McMinn County 197-57 in 1956.

—Staff photo by Gene Pearce
Camden's Danny Boyd—Putting the Check on 104-Total

11

A Time to Trust

by Karla Christian

It was a cold December day as I walked into the mall to begin work at the gift-wrap booth our church was sponsoring during the holiday season. Sounds of Christmas music welcomed me as I opened the door. Colorful lights twinkled as I made my way to our location to begin work. Endeavoring to get into the Christmas spirit, I smiled and greeted the other ladies who were already working.

After several hours of work, I was wrapping a gift for a gentleman when I felt a sharp pain in my head. The pain was so intense that I grabbed the table. As I swayed, the beautiful twinkling lights became blinding lights racing straight toward me. Fortunately, my husband had just walked through the door. We decided that perhaps I just needed some rest and something to eat. However, while eating, my left side became numb, and it was difficult to move my arm and leg. The pain in my head also returned.

My husband insisted that I go to the hospital emergency room. After several tests and an MRI, a neurologist called us to his office and said, "I don't have good news." The scan showed that I had suffered a small aneurysm. Also, for some reason, the lower part of my brain had dropped, blocking the flow of spinal fluid from the cranial cavity and forcing the spinal fluid to attempt to exit through the spinal cord. His prognosis was a continuing deterioration of the nervous system's motor skills, which included walking, playing an instrument, or any other activity of physical coordination. He said the numbness would become worse and that I would not regain the mobility that I had already lost. In his estimation, the enlarging of the spinal cord in the upper thoracic area due to the sustaining pressure of the spinal fluid would someday rupture much like water from a balloon. This would result in one of two consequences: either total paralysis or death. The only recourse was surgery, and the longer we delayed, the more mobility I would lose. The possibility was that therapy rehabilitation would be necessary to deal with the paralysis.

With the doctor's permission, we went ahead with our plans to go home to Texas for Christmas. He warned us that we could not delay the surgery any longer than a month. While in Austin, we consulted another neurosurgeon who agreed with the diagnosis. He felt, however, that surgery should be done immediately, and we agreed with his advice. He explained that he would have to shave my head. On several occasions before the surgery, I kept asking him if it was necessary or if there was another way. "There is no other way," he said. "Surgery is much easier to do without worrying about the hair, and it is much easier to keep infection down when the hair is removed."

But that is not the end of the story, only the beginning. God blessed us with so many wonderful friends who stood with us during this difficult time. We could not have made it without the prayers of the World Network of Prayer, our wonderful church, Heavenview Tabernacle in Winston-Salem, North Carolina, and Christian Life Church in Austin, Texas. And prayer did make the difference.

On January 6, an eight-hour surgery was performed, and God came through for us. The first thing I remember was my wonderful husband standing by my side with Brother Jerry Jones. "Guess what, babe?" he said. "The surgery is over, everything is okay, and you still have your hair." That was good news indeed. The doctor had only shaved the back of my head and left the remainder for me to work with. Immediately I also recognized that I could feel my left foot again and I could move my left arm. That was indeed a miracle! I thank God for allowing this doctor to respond to us in kindness. He utilized his medical skill, but he also made a substantial effort to respect my desires personally.

The diagnosis may seem dire and the outcome ominous, but we have a God who will be with us through every test and trial. Psalm 56:3-4 says, "What time I am afraid, I will trust in thee. In God I will praise his word, in God I have put my trust; I will not fear what flesh can do unto me."

Things have not always been easy, but God is always there to strengthen and guide us through the storms of life. The outcome has been different from what the doctors said. I regained the feeling in my left side, I did not have to attend therapy rehabilitation, and I did get to keep my hair. To God be all the glory!

12

Praise the Lord for His Goodness

by Marvelle Dees

When there is an "overflow" of praise from a grateful heart, God is pleased! No wonder that David was a man after God's own heart. I would join with him in saying, "Oh that men would praise the LORD for his goodness, and for his wonderful works to the children of men!" (This exclamation is repeated four times in Psalm 107.) (In direct contrast, it is noteworthy that unthankfulness is the first step to a reprobate mind (Romans 1:21, 28).)

We know that David had a very grateful heart, because he unceasingly offered praises even when he was in traumatic circumstances. He called it, "sacrificial thanksgiving," verse 22, and added "with rejoicing." In Psalm 103, he commanded his soul to bless the LORD and to forget not all His benefits. Forgetfulness is a forerunner to unthankfulness. The many testimonials in this book will help us to remember to praise and worship our wonderful, miracle-working God! Thank you, Sister Mary Wallace, for taking the time to "put this all together."

Miracles come in different sized packages. We may appraise a miracle as being small or great. But isn't a miracle a miracle? How can any miracle be less than great? Also, miracles occur with variable timings. Some appear to be instantaneous, while others require patient waiting, sometimes for years.

My grandparents had moved next door to us in Cleveland, Texas, where we were pastoring. My grandfather was seventy-nine years old. I was the only grandchild, and he and I had always had a very loving relationship. Growing up, I had spent about as much time with them as with my parents. I was always careful to make no difference between my parents and grandparents. Oh! I loved all of them dearly and could not imagine life without any of them.

As a young girl, I would help my grandfather in his grocery and meat market. My grandmother was my piano teacher and tutor in many ways, but "Papa" was an invisible security blanket for all of us. His strong arms always reached out to me. It was he who dug the grave for my pet kitten and helped with her funeral! Ours was an indescribable bond of love. I had never experienced death with anyone so close to me. So when "Papa" passed away rather suddenly, I was devastated! I could not get relief from the inside pressure of grief. If I could have screamed it out, it would have helped, but praying and crying all seemed to be of no avail. I cannot to this day, fifty years later, describe the pain. Yes, I was now a "grown-up" and a pastor's wife and knew that God is our Comforter, but I could not understand why I was not receiving comfort, especially since Papa was safe at home with the Lord. I was so weak from the lack of sleep and nourishment that my husband said, "You will not be able to attend the second funeral." That was to be in my hometown. I knew that he was right considering the terrible heat and the long drive. What a shame!

I watched as they took his body from the house to the church, and I walked back to my bedroom. As I entered the doorway, instantaneously, all through my being, I felt the healing anointing of the Holy Spirit flow from my head to my toes. Immediately, I was comforted and strengthened with the sweetest calm! I compared it to receiving the Holy Spirit baptism! From that wonderful moment on, grief was an unentertained stranger. The Jesus I had recommended to so many others was now my constant companion, my ever-present Comforter through personal experience!

Many years later, I experienced the same peace and sustaining strength during the loss of my darling grandmother and, then, with both of my parents within a year. In times of perplexity and distress, we have to let the Holy Spirit flow into our emotions. God has performed a lot of miracles in my seventy-nine years, but the miraculous comforting touch is one of the most real and wonderful—past understanding!

A young mother's wail pierced the quietness of a church service in Houston, Texas, where we pastored. She came rushing toward the platform, following her husband, who carried their lifeless young son in his arms. "He's dead! He's dead!" We all started praying. Danny Moreski, an ICU medical assistant, went to the platform to test the child's pulse and vital signs. There was no heartbeat, breathing, or indication of life. We all joined with Brother Dees and the desperate mother, uniting our pleas for a miracle. This continued for eight minutes until life returned to the lifeless form. No more problems. He was sound and well! He is now a grown young man, Steven Montgomery, who remembers that he owes his life to God's miracle-working power. (The same God of II Kings 4:19, 20, 33-35 and Mark 5:35, 39, 42; Malachi 3:6a, and Hebrews 13:8.)

It looked like mumps. It was mumps! But suddenly, Corlis, our young son, became very ill with an extremely high temperature and a terrible headache. He then became unconscious and delirious. His eyes were open, but he no longer recognized his dad or me. He could communicate some, but he was in another world with very little sleep or nourishment. We had always trusted God completely for our healing, but we asked Corlis if he wanted medication. He adamantly replied, "No!" So we continued praying. The church and other ministers bolstered our faith.

On the third night, while my husband was at church, Corlis' condition worsened; he seemed to be verging on seizures. Suddenly death seemed imminent. Then, just as quickly, as we (my mother and Sister Era, who were with me, and of course, Brother Dees and the church) continued in desperate praying, Corlis went into a sound, restful sleep. Instead of death, there was a peaceful calm. The next morning, he awoke a new person, wanting something to eat. When I served him his scrambled egg breakfast, he requested more salt!

Later, I called the doctor to ask how long must one wait following mumps before being allowed to return to school. When I explained Corlis' experience, he exclaimed, "Mrs. Dees, you all must be in tune with the

Man upstairs! Corlis had mumps meningitis!" He further explained that, if a patient lives through it, it could seriously affect the brain. He said that all that anyone could do at this point would be to increase the salt intake! This God had already taken care of the problem by having Corlis desire more salt! Also, I might add that if anything, concerning the brain, his grades improved and his mind was sharper than ever! Furthermore, he definitely remembers that his life belongs to God's will and purpose. We were amazed by it all!

Many years ago when we were pastoring in Cleveland, Texas, our faith was tested in a rather unusual manner. Finances were tight, and my husband had been carefully putting aside a little money to pay our income taxes when due. We were in Lufkin attending the Texas camp meeting when he unexpectedly received a call to go to Louisiana immediately to pick up his father and take him to Houston for eye surgery for cataract removal. It was urgent to save his dad's sight. This consumed our small savings.

Not long afterward, our IRS bill came due. We started praying for God to supply the money. Nothing happened. (At least that we knew of.) Weeks became months. Our prayers got more desperate. Finally the deadline passed and, kind of panicky, I said, "Why don't you just go to the bank and borrow the money?" Patiently but adamantly my husband replied, "No, God is going to provide it." Finally, a cashier's check for the exact amount came from Newfoundland, from a name we did not know! Nothing else was attached! How strange but wonderful just to know that our great, big God was intimately knowledgeable of our particular need!

Months later, Lora Mae (we did not even know her new married name) visited us. She had never done this before nor has ever come again. She shared with us how God had told her to send that amount of money to Brother C. L. Dees! Many years before, Brother Dees had refused to marry her to an unsaved man! She was afraid that her husband would not understand what God instructed her to do, so she kept putting off sending the money. Then one morning when she awoke, God said, "Send the money today!" That was when we had become desperate in prayer!

Does God care? The answer is an emphatic "Yes," even about the smallest matters He cares. That experience happened about fifty-five years ago, but to this present day, when my faith needs an injection of inspiration, I open my treasury of miracles and my memory chants, "He can! He did! He will!" And He does! Again and again.

Miracles have purpose, sometimes dual purpose. Dr. Cooley, a renowned brain surgeon at the large medical center in Houston, gave the family of Foil Bailey no hope. Brother Bailey had suffered a massive heart attack that the doctor said had literally shattered his heart. Brother Bailey was a good man but weak and wavering in his relationship with God. His pastor, my husband, felt led to tell his wife, "We can't let Brother Bailey meet God as he is. I'm going to pray, and if he lives through tonight, he will live." She readily agreed. Brother Bailey lived through the night and was healed! God extended his life twelve years. He went back to work, resumed his hobby of fishing, and was faithful to God and the church. In fact, he was enjoying a Texas camp meeting when the Lord took him home to glory. Brother Dees didn't even have time to get to the hospital.

In retrospect, this miracle healing was four-fold in purpose: Dr. Cooley witnessed a miracle. Brother Bailey's life was extended twelve years. No telling how many lives he touched. He was ready to go and God received the glory!

Even as I am writing this story, my memory is refreshing me with more awesome wonders of which I am a personal witness. Hebrews 11:32 says, "And what more shall I say? for the time would fail me to tell of. . . ." Mary Wallace did not request that I write a book—only a chapter! But, please, just one more miracle.

Missionary Robert Nix and his wife, Sue, desired a child so much that they requested Brother Dees to anoint and pray for them to have a child. He did, and they left for their field of labor, Peru. God gave them four fine sons. Jokingly we said that we might have to pray for them to stop having babies since they were being born so quickly. All four sons are now ministers—Kevin, Keith, and Kelly are foreign missionaries, and one is an American pastor. Just think how many precious souls that may not have been reached had God not performed that one miracle. God is so good! And sometimes He surprises us.

Finally, whether our needs are small or great, God is touched with the feeling of our infirmities (Hebrews 4:15). Our God is a miracle-working God!

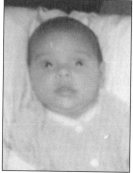

Steven Montgomery
as infant

Steven, high school

Rev. D. L. and Marvelle Dees

Steven, six-years-old

13

Little Things Mean a Lot

by Lynda Allison Doty

*S*ometimes those "little things" can make a difference in a weary person's day. Little things, like a cup of tea or a word of encouragement. And sometimes those little answers to prayers speak to us again of our Father's great love and care for us.

There was a time when my children and I were, in effect, homeless and wandering about the country with no real place to go. This happened to be by God's design, for during this time, I was what I like to call "half-born"; I had the Holy Ghost but had not yet heard of Jesus Name baptism. God was leading this hungry lady to the church where He wanted me to have my sins remitted in the waters of baptism.

A woman alone on the roads with two children can often be in a dangerous, precarious position. There was the time, for example, when we had to make a trip to another town about seventy miles away. Our gas tank was absolutely empty. I did not have the money to put gas in it—in fact, we had parked it with the intention of not driving again until I found work in this new town. Yet the Lord asked us to travel to this community to witness to a person we had met earlier. We prayed about it, and my son Joseph said, "Mom, if God said to do it, we'd better do it." And so we set out on fumes alone.

We had traveled the seventy miles and reached the outskirts of town, when the car quit. We coasted to the side of the road, got out, and prayed for someone to come along who would help us get safely to our destination in that town.

As we sat on the side of the road, a car slowed down, and it looked for all the world like the driver would stop. He was close enough that I saw him clearly, an old farmer man. Then without warning, he sped up again and chugged on down the highway. A few minutes later another car came along. This one stopped, assessed the problem, and offered to push our car to the nearest gas station and also offered to buy us a tank of gas! When we arrived there, I began to fill the car with gasoline.

As I stood there at the pump, I happened to spot the old farmer man who had almost stopped. I ran over to him and asked him why he had not stopped. This is what he said: "Well, ma'am, when I saw that big guy with you, I decided you didn't need my help, so I came on into town."

Big guy? The kids and I looked at each other. There had been no "big guy" with us! What had this farmer man seen?

Whatever happened that day, we arrived safely at our destination, witnessed to the lady, and returned home with a full tank of gas! When we obey God, He will take care of us! He answers our littlest prayers!

Here are the three of us—
fresh off the road and settled in a church!

14

The Power of the Name

by Linda Allison Doty

There have been times over the years when the unction to use the name of Jesus came upon me in a moment of danger. I soon learned that, although there was no time to fall on my knees, this was a most powerful prayer!

The first time I remember was when my children and I had befriended a woman who was being abused by her husband. She and her children were staying in our home for safety. The husband found out where they were, and he decided to come to force them to go home. We were all in the yard when he walked up. The look in his eyes could be described as nothing but devilish, and he focused upon his wife. She refused to go with him, and he became irate. Instead of going for her, though, he decided to come after the one who had befriended her: me. He began uttering threats and charged toward me, those dark, evil eyes piercing me. That unction came upon me, and I pointed toward him, "In Jesus' name, stop!" He froze, fear suddenly clouding his face.

Then he turned and hurried out of the yard the same way he came.

Another time, my children and I had just moved into a new house and were not familiar with the neighborhood. My daughter had left her pet white rabbit on the front porch while she made a place for him inside. As we all worked around the house, we suddenly heard the sound of a low, ugly growl. It was coming from the front porch! We raced toward the sound and saw a huge dog, moving hungrily toward Julie's rabbit. That creature was actually salivating! The look of terror on my daughter's face was pitiful, and without thinking, I moved onto the porch. The anointing came upon me. I pointed at the dog and said, "Stop! In Jesus' name!" And that furry critter began to cower and back away.

The last I would like to mention was when I was living at the church on Canal Street in New Orleans. I wanted to travel back to South Carolina to spend Thanksgiving with my sister and decided to rent a more comfortable car for the trip. The rental agency was only two blocks down Canal Street, and it was eight o'clock in the morning. The street was heavy with traffic. Feeling safe, I set out to walk the two blocks to the agency.

At the end of the first block, as I crossed in front of a large service station, two men began to move toward me. I could see from their eyes that I was indeed their target and that they were of evil intent. As they continued toward me, the back of my neck began to tingle. Suddenly, I felt that unction, turned and faced them, and pointed that finger. I did not say a word, but the Holy Ghost was there, and they both fell backward onto the pavement. Confused, they scrambled to their feet and took off running!

15

Don't Close Those Doors!

by Lynda Allison Doty

od had provided us with a lovely little storefront for the home missions work we were starting. The rent was good, but, unfortunately, the handful of people we had was not getting the rent paid. We knew we could not continue paying it out of our limited personal income.

One Sunday, just before service, the roof in the back part of the building caved in. At this point, we saw no alternative except to give up the building and move the church back into our living room. We discussed the move with our home missions director, who had not as yet visited our little church. He came the following week to help us move the furnishings into a storage unit.

When he arrived and saw the beautiful building with the low rent, he said he just couldn't see giving it up. He slipped off, made a few phone calls, and came back to tell us that the district would pay our rent for the rest of the year! And he would personally come to help repair the damages!

View of the interior of our little storefront church.

One of the front windows, entering our little church. Reaching out to Winnsboro!

16

Fearfully Made: Sonnie's Story

by Virginia Douglas

*G*od does indeed answer prayer and sees every church of His—big and small!

"I will praise thee; for I am fearfully and wonderfully made: marvellous are thy works; and that my soul knoweth right well" (Psalm 139:14). The story of Sonnie illustrates the perfection of God's careful oversight of each of our lives. "The darkness and the light are both alike to thee" (Psalm 139:12).

Hidden in Mother's skirts, little Sonnie (pronounced like Bonnie) sought refuge. Her arms wrapped tightly around the solid leg while her mother, embarrassed in front of a stranger, reached back to pull her out with a pinching grip. "Mom's skirts couldn't protect me from emotional threat, but there was that momentary sense of safety when I was hiding behind her with her skirt wrapped around me."

And how Sonnie needed a sense of security! As long as

she could remember, fear dominated her days and terrorized her nights. She was too little to name the evil that threatened her little world. Imaginary playmates appeared to console her. Each one had a name and each one had a seat at the dinner table. Her imaginary playmates never criticized or taunted her. They sympathized with her and assured her that she was not the problem; other people were mean.

When the day came that she had to go to school, Sonnie was paralyzed with fear. Her mother stayed in the classroom with her for two days, and then she was left to deal with it as best she could. "Everything about school scared me. My biggest daily thought was 'How do I get out of here and get home?'"

As time went on, her world expanded beyond her parents' home. The need for imaginary playmates passed. She figured out what pleased people and how to avoid their displeasure or anger.

She was glad when friends invited her to church. By the time Sonnie reached adolescence, she was an ecumenical disciple. "I was baptized in the Baptist church, taught in the Lutheran church, and confirmed in the Covenant church."

Hidden in the guise of sweetness, Sonnie pursued approval as a compliant student in college. Like her mother's skirts, approving comments and smiles wrapped her in a momentary refuge. Internal conflict reigned; she needed others to supply approval while fearing they would not accept her.

Trying with all her might to balance her world with good behavior, her tender feelings were easily hurt. If she were embarrassed, deprived of approval, or criticized even slightly, anxiety would rise like a tornado to demolish every good thought. "The humiliation would run like a recorder in my head. It got so bad that my only stability was to tell myself, 'In three days, I will be able to think about something else.'"

She graduated from college and worked for a couple of years before marriage. Like many anxious people, she learned all the good habits of successful, likeable people. She enjoyed praise of her job performance.

The people around her, including her husband, couldn't see the terrible internal taskmaster. Their first son came in thirteen months. Sonnie chose to leave her job and stay home with her baby.

Hidden in her own home with a good husband and a child, she believed she should be content and fulfilled. Instead, she sank into a deep depression. Fleeing to the desert around her home in Las Vegas, alone and brooding, she thought, "If this is the best, I might as well do myself in." She was so miserable that she was willing to give up her life. God came to mind, but her heart was cold.

Hope

Her husband agreed that she needed a break. She went to her sister's in Oregon. There she learned that her sister's life had been completely changed by God. Her sister had received the Holy Ghost. A couple of sentences of her sister's testimony took root in Sonnie's mind. The first was, "Jesus can actually change your life!" Hope was instilled immediately. Maybe she, too, could live a fearless life in Christ!

Her sister's second penetrating statement was, "You are your own worst enemy." This opened the way to repentance. Pleasing people would never eliminate her fears. "The antidote to fear is the fear of the Lord," her sister said.

On the flight home, the Spirit nudged Sonnie to take a new look at the familiar spirit of fear that wrapped her soul in dirty swaddling clothes—self-pity and victimization—like a neglected infant. Those old voices of childhood had instilled lies.

The Hiding Place

Sonnie returned home with new hope, not in a new mental device but in a new life. Billy Graham was on television the night of her return from Oregon. She responded to the invitation to turn her life over to Jesus Christ. She recognized that it would be a total commitment of her life to Christ. She would stake everything on His promise to save her.

Her sister had given her the book by Corrie ten Boom, *The Hiding Place*. Sonnie stayed up to read the book through the night. She read about the German invasion of Holland. Corrie ten Boom wrote that "there are no ifs in God's world. And no places that are safer than other places. The center of His will is our only safety."

Sonnie woke free of the obsessive self-annihilating tapes. The tape recorder in her head had been silenced. "It was at that moment that the Lord delivered me from the false consolation of self-protection that had been sown in my heart by the voices of my lonely early childhood. That was the beginning of the transformational healing."

She denounced that old spirit of self-pity. The voices of her childhood were not friendly but deceptive. Sonnie experienced a deep desire to love God with all her heart, soul, mind, and strength.

"From the beginning of the time when the Lord said very clearly that He was going to heal me, He also made it clear that repentance was going to be a big part of the process. As I began to ask Him for healing and deliverance from fear, He made it clear that I also needed to confess the unbelief and lack of trust of Him, which were the actual issues behind the fear. It was a matter of admitting and recognizing that I was helpless to change myself yet being very clear that repentance and doing the work of facing the issues, praying, and inviting others to pray for me were my part of the bargain."

Sonnie and her husband found a church. Her husband had been brought up in the Lutheran church but had not found a personal faith until they joined a band of Pentecostal believers. He went on to the ministry. They pastored a new work in Las Vegas. Her walk with God grew richer through the ensuing passages of her life as mother, pastor's wife, and member of the body of Christ. The trials that go with life would continue to keep Sonnie in prayer, living on God's promises. She noted the words of Frances Roberts:

"Look to Me, My child, and all your needs will be met by My abundant provision. I will not suffer the enemy to overthrow him who puts his confidence in Me. I am faithful to My Word, and I have promised never to fail nor to forsake. Obedience is the fabric of happiness."

All emotional healing begins at the foot of the cross of Jesus Christ. In Psalm 34:4, the Spirit of Jesus counseled Sonnie: "I sought the LORD, and he heard me, and delivered me from all my fears." In verse 18, His love touched her, "The LORD is nigh unto them that are of a broken heart; and saveth such as be of a contrite spirit."

Sonnie went on to seminary and recently completed her master's in theology. She labors to help others on the way to emotional healing. Education about family dynamics and the development of emotional problems helps put in perspective the suffering and trouble that are part of life. "And the point is—not that our parents' faults had no effect—those are very real—but Satan would have us believe that all unhappiness is the fault of others. The enemy tries to instill, from infancy, self-pity and victimization. He wants us to take no responsibility.

"We become our own worst enemy unless we turn and repent. What my story says, and what your story says, is that 'It's never too late to turn to Jesus.' In His infinite mercy, knowing these broken experiences we are made of, that we are dust, He permits us to protect ourselves as best we can until we turn to the fullness of His love, the fullness of His grace." In the hiding place in Christ (Colossians 3:3) who is our life, we continue until His appearing.

Virginia Douglas, author with grandchildren, Billy and Bekkah, 1999.

Sonnie at age 4

Sonnie at age 5, 1950

17

The Story of Jimmy Ray Sanders

by Douglas Ellingsworth

irefighters dug feverishly through the splintered furniture and twisted metal strewn in the ravine. The nose of the trailer was smashed into the muddy creek bank; its rear wheels, stuck on the edge of the bridge high above, held it almost vertical. The load of furniture had been shoved through the front of the trailer and through the cab of the big truck that was pulling it. The force pushed the cab of the truck away from the trailer but crushed the engine and driver's seat under the trailer and much of its cargo.

The rescue workers had managed to free the driver who, although badly injured, managed to tell them a second man was riding with him. It was this man whom they now scrambled to find.

Trucking, drinking, and drugs had not always been Jimmy Sanders' life. He grew up in an Apostolic church, reared by loving parents who were faithful ministers of the gospel. As a young man, Jimmy felt the Lord speak to him and accepted his call into the ministry. But, as is too often the case, other things seemed to become more important, and Jimmy was no longer attending church.

Jimmy became a truck driver and for many years hauled loads all across the United States. His drinking and drug use soon became an addiction. Jimmy had slipped far from the life he had enjoyed as a young man.

Although Jimmy stopped praying and going to church, his mother never did. Her son remained constantly in her thoughts and prayers. Fearful that he might lose his life before coming back to God, she made him a special blanket to carry in his truck. She didn't tell him, but inside the blanket she sewed a special cloth that had been prayed over. She and others had prayed earnestly that God would keep Jimmy safe as he traveled and that God's mercy would bring him to salvation.

Those prayers had to be what protected Jimmy when he fell asleep early that morning as he drove though eastern Oklahoma. His eighteen-wheeler drifted off I-40 and flew 106 feet in the air before crashing cab-first into a creek bank. The cab and the load crushed around him. Firefighters worked for over an hour getting him out of the wreckage. The only part of the cab of that truck that was not completely crushed was the small section that cradled Jimmy's body. Barely alive, he was badly injured.

Jimmy was rushed to a hospital in Fort Smith, Arkansas, where he was placed on life support. His upper body had taken a severe beating. Along with broken arms and ribs, he suffered from massive head injuries. The medical team called his family together, explained the severity of his injuries, and tried to prepare them for his impending death.

As news of the accident spread, Jimmy's name was

placed on prayer lists all over the country. For four weeks, Jimmy lay in the hospital, kept alive by feeding tubes and machines. His family gathered by his side, and, aided by wonderful local Apostolics, they had never met before, prayed continually for his salvation.

The doctors continued to advise the family that it was unlikely that Jimmy would survive. His injuries were simply too severe for him to overcome. While Jimmy's family may not have understood all of the medical terms the doctors used, they certainly knew the power of the Lord they served. So they were excited, but not too surprised, when four weeks after his accident, Jimmy regained consciousness!

Neither were they shocked the day the doctors said that he was well enough to be transported to a medical center near his home in Tennessee. "But," they warned, "realize he will be confined to a rehabilitation center for at least two years." He would have to learn how to walk and care for himself all over again.

Elated with his progress, Jimmy's family was excited to have him close to home. They, along with all the churches they had contacted, continued to pray for Jimmy's recovery and salvation. What a jubilant family gathered around when Jimmy walked out of the rehab hospital! He was released after just two weeks of treatment!

A few days after he was released from the rehab center, Jimmy went to church with his family. Before the preacher finished his message, Jimmy stepped out of his pew and walked toward the altar. He never made it to the front. There in the middle of the aisle, he repented and God gloriously filled him with the Holy Ghost! Not only did God bring him back from the edge of death, but He also delivered Jimmy from the alcohol and drugs that had controlled his life.

In the weeks that followed, members of Jimmy's family, witnesses to miracles they could never deny, began attending church with him. His wife soon received the Holy Ghost. One son-in-law, who had been raised as a Catholic, is now filled with the Holy Ghost. While Jimmy still suffers from some of the effects of the accident (such as short-term memory loss), he tells of God's healing power every chance he gets.

Those firefighters and rescue workers never did find that second man they were frantically searching for at the accident scene. They called Jimmy's house and asked his wife who usually rode with him. They called the trucking company and asked who was assigned as his partner. Both times they were told that Jimmy drove alone and never allowed anyone to ride with him. Assuming that Jimmy was just talking "out of his head," they gave up the search. But Jimmy knows! That man he saw just before he crashed had to be an angel—sent by God in response to a prayer cloth sewn inside a blanket by a mother who understood the power of prayer!

18

Through the Storm

by Roffie Ensey

he optometrist looked into my eyes and said, "You don't even need glasses! However, you do have a problem that I am not qualified to handle, so I am going to send you to an ophthalmologist and have him evaluate you."

This was in the late summer of 1969, and we were living in St. Louis. In 1967 my husband became the general secretary of the Home Missions Division, and we moved to St. Louis to assume those responsibilities. I was twenty-seven years old, with two children—Randy, seven, and Debbie, four.

My storm started with a loss of hearing. Shortly after this episode, I began to have severe headaches. At first they were manageable but quickly reached the place of being unbearable. The doctor I went to for the headaches gave me some very strong pain medicine. However, even this would not stop the pain for very long. All it did was ease the pain a little and put me to sleep for a while. After about two hours, the pain would return with a vengeance and wake me from a deep sleep.

With two small children, it was not easy to keep going when I felt so bad all of the time. Just getting out of bed was a major chore. Randy was in the first grade, my husband had to be at work by eight o'clock, and Debbie was still at home with me.

Then my equilibrium began to go. Many times just walking across the floor, I would fall. We lived in the second-story flat of an old house in South St. Louis that was built before the turn of the century. One day someone rang the doorbell, and when I started down the stairs to answer the door, I fell into a window on the landing. It was a stained glass window with metal strips, and thankfully it did not give way. If it had broken, I would have fallen about twenty feet to the street below, probably to my death.

My hair began to be a major concern because it was breaking off and falling out. I was losing my "glory" and did not know what to do about it. During this time, I consulted several doctors. One of them told me, after a complete exam, that he could find nothing wrong with me. He said I was losing muscle tone and that jogging a couple of miles each day would help. I wondered how I could jog when I could not walk without stumbling.

I began to have double vision that made it difficult to do the normal things a mother needs to do. Just going to the grocery store was a major chore. I could not walk down the aisles in the store and see what I needed with just a glance. I would have to stop to allow time for my eyes to focus on each product before I could tell what it was.

I wore glasses, so I decided that perhaps needing my

98

glasses changed caused my headaches. The optometrist referred me to an ophthalmologist. When the ophthalmologist looked into my eyes, he said, "Yes, you do have a problem, but it is out of my field. You need to see a neurologist. Let me call my friend and see when he can examine you."

The date for my appointment with the neurologist was September 2, 1969. This was the latter part of August, so I had a few days to wait. During this time, the headaches were unbearable. I would take the strongest medication the doctors could give me, and the pain would subside for only about two hours. Then I would have two hours of excruciating pain before I could take anything else.

After a brief examination, which included sticking sharp needles into my face, the neurologist said, "I want you to go straight to the Barnes Medical Center. I will call and make arrangements." He evidently knew something was terribly wrong.

In the hospital, I was turned over to Dr. Schwartz, a neurosurgeon who taught brain surgery at the medical college in St. Louis. After several days of intense testing, X-rays, CAT scans, dye tests, and hearing tests, I was taken back to my room. My husband, who stayed by my side through it all, decided to go back to his office for a while. After he left, Dr. Schwartz came to my room to tell me what he had found. I was alone when he broke the news. I am sure he did not expect the response he got from me when he said, "Roffie, we have found your problem. You have a brain tumor. It is such a shame for a young woman like you to have this."

At that time, just when I needed it, God gave me a

99

calm and a peace that cannot be described. The peace of God that transcends understanding flooded my soul.

Dr. Schwartz evidently expected me to fall apart, and when I didn't, he continued: "Your tumor is very large and in an extremely difficult place to get to. It is underneath the cerebellum, pressing against the brain stem, and wrapped around a nerve. It is operable. However, if you live through the surgery, you could be a vegetable for the rest of your life. Or you could be paralyzed, either partially or fully. There could be brain damage. At best you will have memory loss and may have to learn all the basics again—how to walk, talk, read, and so forth." (We learned later that virtually any time the brain is touched there is some damage done.)

Evidently Dr. Schwartz was not getting the response from me he expected, so he said, "Young lady, where is your husband? I need to talk with him!" My husband had gone back to work, so I gave Dr. Schwartz his phone number. He called him to come in for consultation. I am sure Dr. Schwartz got the reaction he was looking for from my husband. It is always easier to go through something yourself than to watch someone you love go through it.

I think Dr. Schwartz thought the brain tumor must have already affected my mind. My mind had been affected by something, but it was not the tumor. It was parents who taught me that God has His way in the storm, and you can trust Him!

I learned a valuable lesson that day. I learned that God does not give us strength to fight imaginary battles. We often wonder what we would do in a given situation, even thinking through a certain scenario and living it out in our mind. But grace comes at the time it is needed, never early or late. It is in the heat of the real battle that we receive strength and divine enablement.

The only thing that really brought tears to my eyes during this whole ordeal was the day they shaved my head. That is still a very painful memory because they took away my "glory," all except for a little tuft right in front.

When they came to the room to tell us they were ready to take me down to shave my head, Mother and my sister braided my hair in two braids and cut them off while we all cried. I still have those braids as a reminder.

A nurse then shaved my head as clean as a man's face. After that a doctor came in and drilled a hole in the top of my head and took out a piece of bone the size of a nickel. This was done to relieve the pressure on my brain. I was scheduled for surgery the next morning.

The day I went to surgery, the nurse who took me down cried all the way. I kept trying to tell her everything would be okay, but she had taken many patients to this kind of surgery before, and she knew how it would be—or thought she knew. Her confidence was in the doctors. But I was not putting my confidence in man who had only studied about the brain; my confidence was in the One who made the brain. He would not fail me. He was the One in control!

They needed to do one last test before surgery to help them pinpoint exactly where the tumor was. They strapped me in a chair that looked much like an electric chair with a hole in the back where my spine was. They took ten cubic centimeters of fluid from my spine and put in ten cubic centimeters of air, then turned me upside down to allow the air to surround the tumor.

X-rays were taken to determine the exact location and size of the tumor. This took much longer than they had expected and was tremendously painful. I found out later the reason it took so long was that they could not believe what they were seeing. The tumor was much larger than they had originally estimated. The tumor was indeed in a delicate place, under the cerebellum, and it was the size of a very large lemon or a small pear!

From there I went to surgery. The surgery took seven and one-half hours. When it was finished, the anesthesiologist began talking to me to wake me. I opened my eyes in the operating room and said, "Give me a blanket—I am cold!" They were not expecting any audible response at this point, much less a rational request.

One of the men in the operating room came to see me a few days later and told me, "We have never had anybody come out of that kind of surgery talking like you did."

When they took the tumor out, they also took the eighth nerve around which the tumor had grown, leaving the left side of my face paralyzed. I could not close my left eye, and the tear ducts could not provide moisture for that eye, leaving it very dry.

After a brief time in recovery, they put me in ICU and allowed my family to come in one at a time. I am sure it was quite a shock for them to see me in such a terrible condition. My shaved head was covered with an antiseptic medicine the color of ocher and swathed in bandages. There was a clear plastic cover over my eye, attached to a rubber band that was around my head. This left eye could not be closed, so I lay there with one eye open and one eye closed.

My family had been warned that I probably would not know them and would not be able to talk. But as each of them came in, I recognized my visitor. I called each of them by name and talked with them.

My husband came in first, and I asked him if he had called the people we promised to call after surgery. He looked at me with a little grin and said, "No, I don't have their phone numbers with me."

I said, "If you have a pen and paper, I'll give you their numbers!" And I did. (Remember, I was not expected to be able to talk or have a memory capacity for this!)

On the second day in ICU, I looked around me at the thirteen patients with whom I shared this ward. We were all brain surgery patients, and I was the only one who was alert and rational. The rest of them were either in a comatose state or out of their head and just jabbering.

As I began to think of how good God was and what He had already done for me, the tears began to flow. I say "tears," but actually it was only one tear because of the paralysis in the left side of my face. A single tear slipped down my right cheek, and I began to sing softly to myself.

My bed was positioned near the nurse's station, with her desk almost at the foot of my bed. When I began to sing, she looked over the rim of her glasses at me. You could almost read her thoughts: "We have been waiting for this, and here it is. She has really gone off the deep end this time."

I sang . . .

Till the storm passes over and the thunder sounds no
    more,
Till the clouds roll forever from the sky,

Hold me fast, let me stand in the hollow of Thy hand.
Keep me safe till this storm passes by.

Later I realized that this is just what He did.

Doctors had told us that the third day after brain surgery the brain swells. When my family came in to see me that morning, the chaplain met them and told them, "This is the critical day. We could lose her, so don't be surprised at what you find. You may want to stop by the chapel before you go up."

So while my family was in the chapel praying, Dr. Schwartz came to see me in ICU. After talking with me a few minutes, he asked me if I would be willing to go to a doctors' conference in the hospital auditorium. He said they would take me down on a gurney. He wanted the other doctors to see me because this was the result they would like to see in all their brain surgery patients. I agreed to go to the meeting on one condition: that he would get me out of ICU. He promised to find me a room and have me moved right away.

At the conference, I talked with numerous doctors, interns, and medical students. They examined me and talked with me for about an hour, marveling at my progress. When they wheeled me back to ICU, the nurse confirmed that they had found a room for me. Of course I was ready to go right then, so I asked what we were waiting for. She informed me that someone would be along with a wheelchair soon since I was not able to walk.

I replied, "Oh, I believe I can. Let's go!" With a little help from my husband, I got out of bed and walked! God is still in control!

So, after three days rather than three weeks in ICU,

they moved me to my own room. I was so happy to be out of ICU. It was so cold in there, and the doctor would not let me get warm for fear of infection. They never turned the lights out and it was also very noisy, making it difficult to rest. Now I could rest without lights in my one eye that would not close.

Two weeks after they removed the tumor, I was back in surgery. This time it was for a nerve transplant. During the first surgery, they had to cut the eighth nerve that controls the left side of my face and my hearing. This transplant would only serve to help me close my eye and relax my face a little. It would never completely replace the one that was severed.

Dr. Schwartz explained, "If we take the nerve out of her tongue, she will have to learn to talk again. Half of her tongue will atrophy, possibly leaving her with a permanent speech impediment. She will be able to close her left eye with a movement of her tongue. We know she has done everything we said she could not do, but this time will be different. She will not be able to speak for a while, and she will always have a speech impediment."

They actually cut my ear almost off and went through to my tongue and took a nerve. Then they transplanted the nerve behind my left ear, explaining that its growth would provide some movement and life, but it would never totally replace the nerve that had been severed.

This was another seven and one-half hour surgery. Before going into surgery this time, I asked Dr. Schwartz to allow me to go back to my room rather than ICU if the surgery went well.

I was placed in recovery for a while and then sent to ICU. As they were wheeling me down the hall, I asked where they were taking me. When the nurse said ICU, I said, "No, I don't belong in there." Of course she thought I did not know what I was talking about. (Remember, I am not supposed to even be able to talk at this time!)

When we stopped outside ICU, the head nurse heard the commotion and came out to see what was going on. The nurse's aid wheeling me down told her, "She says she does not belong in here, but she just came out of seven and one-half hours of surgery."

The head nurse looked at my chart and barked, "She *doesn't* belong in here. Take her to her room!" In situations like this, one learns to be thankful for small favors.

The next morning a little before eight, I was sitting up in bed with all the tubes and IVs out, talking on the phone! This was only about eleven hours after surgery.

When my husband answered the phone and heard my voice, he began to cry. I asked him what was wrong. Then he told me what the doctor had told him: I was not supposed to be able to talk for a while and then not without a speech impediment.

Two weeks later, I went home after four weeks in the hospital. This was just a few days before my twenty-eighth birthday. It was wonderful to be outside and to see the beautiful fall colors in St. Louis.

The God we serve is altogether trustworthy. He does all things well! Today, thirty-five years later with His help, I am still going strong. To the only wise God, the One who is able to do exceeding abundantly above all we can ask or think, be all the glory and honor now and forevermore!

Roffie Ensey, after surgery, 1969

Jerry & Roffie Ensey

Debbie & Randy Ensey, St. Louis, Missouri, 1969

19

The Miracle of Positioning Men

by Fred J. Foster

*T*exas Bible College in the '60s became a fantastic training center, with an enrollment of four hundred, for the propagation of the gospel of Jesus Christ. No one knew in its formation how strong it would become and how it would train so many great leaders for the future of the United Pentecostal Church International from its campus in Houston, Texas. Alumni include Wayne Huntley, pastor, conference, and camp meeting speaker, and former North Carolina District Superintendent; Mark Jordan, pastor and District Superintendent of Ohio; C. Patton Williams, pastor and Florida District Superintendent; David Mathis, former District Superintendent in the Dakotas; Wilma Nix, former missionary to Africa; Jimmy Hayes, former Superintendent of the Texico District; the Wendells, who were the first missionaries to Ethiopia, to name only a few pastors, evangelists, district and national leaders, and missionaries who came from that time.

This is not a story to promote one college above

another as I am at this writing the president of Jackson College of Ministries in Jackson, Mississippi. But it is a testimony of the miraculous working of God in a young preacher's life to help bring to pass a great instrument in the hand of God. I believe God works miracles such as these to put people into position to accomplish His will.

I was pastoring in my old hometown of Albuquerque, New Mexico, in the 1950s, where we had gone to found a new church in 1954. My wife, Pat, and I had three preschool boys, Mark, Tom, and Tim. We prayed and reached out to the community, and in carrying this new church burden and in prayer, I had a tremendous impression to found a Bible college. In the beginning, I felt this to be an impossibility for me to do. My wife and I were in our late twenties and pastoring in a geographical location far from the Pentecostal population. We had few churches in New Mexico in those years, and it didn't seem to be a good place at that time for a college. I tried to put it aside, but the burden would not go away but persisted in my prayers.

The First Miracle

In talking to the Lord, I told Him that if He wanted me to be involved in founding a new Bible college, He would have to work the miracles to bring it to pass. To my amazement over the next few years, I saw Him do just that.

As the first miracle, in September 1958, the First United Pentecostal Church of Orange, Texas, invited my family and me to become their pastoral family. What a miracle that was! I was a young unknown preacher just thirty-one years old and only seven years out of Bible college. The Orange church was one of the larger in the Texas District, and it seemed impossible for an unknown young man from New Mexico, whom the superintendent and presbyter had not heard of, to be able to suddenly become the pastor of this great church. I have always attributed this to God's miraculous work on the way to Texas Bible College.

The Second Miracle

The Texas District had their annual conference in the Port Arthur Labor Union Hall in the spring of 1959. Port Arthur was seventeen miles from Orange, where I pastored in southeast Texas. In those days, preachers did not know who would be preaching the night services. They were chosen usually during the day before the night he was to preach. Doyle Spears, who pastored in Longview, Texas, was the first night speaker and did an outstanding job.

At the end of the next afternoon's business, District Superintendent V. A. Guidroz called my name and said I would be preaching that night. Naturally I was shocked. Many had heard of me by now because of my taking the pastorate at Orange, but none had ever heard me preach. I'm sure there was some speculation and wondering how I would do. Certainly I was among their number.

Thankfully I was only a few miles from my church study. God came through for me. Although in my wildest dreams never thinking I would be called on to preach, I was inspired on the way across the high Rainbow Bridge over the Neches River with what to preach. It was a miracle within a miracle. I felt God gave me confidence that He was giving me something for this conference. All these things were miracles that would bring about a great college.

That night God anointed in a wonderful way to bring blessing as He alone can do. He not only brought blessing to that particular service but also brought notice to an unknown preacher. He was giving a certain regard to someone so confidence would be in the minds of the ministerial constituency for the future work. It was a miracle of God.

The Third Miracle

I decided I wanted to cast my bread upon the water, so I said, "Let's start a Saturday morning Bible college for area preachers and saints." I knew it would be important to get District Superintendent V. A. Guidroz's blessing. Not knowing him well, I asked my friend, *Texas Sentinel* editor Murray Burr, who was very close to Brother Guidroz, to talk to him about it. Murray Burr was highly influential in the district, and having his and the superintendent's blessing would give us a great send-off. God allowed Brother Burr to come through with V. A. Guidroz's approval. Naturally I was very happy, so we kicked it off with the helpful leadership and teaching of high school principal Paul Willis. A number of people were blessed by the Saturday morning sessions. Another miracle of God.

The Climate in the Texas District

There had been a college in the Texas District in the past at a place called Mountain Top. This school was moved to Hillsboro later. For several years, quite a few Texans had been educated there, but for varied reasons, the college was closed in the late '40s. In discussing the possibilities of starting a college, I found favorable feelings toward it. The superintendent was a visionary, which lent hope to the possibility. Also, a large group of preachers my age, a little younger or a little older, had great progressive faith in taking the gospel around the world. Men like J. T. Pugh, James Gilbert, James Kilgore, Hulen Myre, Titus McDonald, O. W. Williams, Oliver Fauss, Arless Glass, Orlan Ray Fauss, Forrest Ford, Murray Burr, I, and others saw that it could probably be accomplished. The climate seemed very friendly toward bringing a Bible college into fruition.

Another Miracle

The annual sectional conference of Section One in the winter of 1962 was held in Pastor King's church in Beaumont. Allen Doyle was the presbyter, and I was the secretary. At this conference, Murray Burr and I brought a resolution with the intent of our section to send a resolution to the spring district conference for the explicit vote to found a college in the district. It was unanimously passed.

On to District Conference

The conference that spring was held in Kilgore, Texas. I remember very well when the resolution was brought to the floor. Coming out of our section, I felt I should introduce the first argument in its behalf. Surprisingly, there was no argument against it. Questions, yes, of how we could get it on its way, but nothing to throw cold water on the idea. Another miracle that had to come to pass was getting V. A. Guidroz on board. He was a dynamic leader and influential throughout all the ministers and churches of Texas. Without his support, it most likely would not fly. The miracle happened. Brother Guidroz became one of the college's biggest proponents. So we were on our way.

One Last Miracle in This Part of My Life

After a college board was chosen, of which I was one of the members, we put everything together to get the college started. We now needed a president. I felt all through this process that God wanted me to be that person, but it would be up to the board. The district did know that I had been instrumental in bringing the idea of a college, but they did have their own favorite son. I had only been in the district a few short years, and I knew it would be a miracle of God if I were chosen. The favorite son, rightfully so a great man and highly respected in Texas and throughout the UPCI, was J. T. Pugh. When the presidency was offered to him, he turned it down in my favor. When I was asked to take it, I had no hesitancy. I knew this was the will of God. It had been working through the years, and now the impossibility in my younger life in New Mexico was miraculously coming to pass in Texas. We officially announced the opening and that I would be president at a specially called district conference at the summer camp meeting in June 1963 with the opening classes in January 1964. To God be the glory! He is a miracle-working God. He allowed me to be president until January 1970, when I accepted the pastorate of the West Monroe, Louisiana, church.

Conclusion

God has a plan in His purpose for our lives. We can believe that He is working in our everyday affairs to bring His plan to pass. As we persevere and stay faithful to Him, He will be able to use us. He will make us a blessing where we are while positioning us for His ultimate goal.

20

A Miracle

by Paul & Patty Gordon

y wife, Patty, and I had one daughter, nine-year-old Bethany. We had been trying for several years to have another child. There had been numerous prayers, doctor's visits, procedures, and two traumatic miscarriages.

In January 2000, Patty found out she was pregnant again. On one of her first doctor's visits, they found the counts high, indicating pregnancy. However, upon further testing, the doctor could not detect a heartbeat, which he indicated he should hear with counts that high. When Patty and I visited with the doctor on that Friday afternoon in late January, he said the baby was dead, it was another early miscarriage. He suggested that a D & C procedure be scheduled for that following Monday.

In our discussion with the doctor, we were hesitant to act too quickly. This hesitancy must have come from the Lord. We asked if we could wait a week and have another ultrasound. He said we could, but it wouldn't make any difference; the results would be the same. He had never been wrong before.

We left the doctor's office distraught. I dropped Patty off at our home. I didn't want to believe that this was God's will.

I went up the road to Patty's grandmother and aunt's house to tell them what the doctor had said. Seeing my devastation, Grandma said, "Paul, we can fast and pray about this if you want to believe for a miracle. The doctor, though a competent man, does not know the God we serve." That's what I needed to hear. I needed somebody who would have faith and trust God with me. So that's what we decided to do.

I later called Patty's former pastor, Brother Lester Thompson. He was retired and wintering in Florida. He encouraged me by telling me about miracles he had witnessed in his life. He also said that he and Sister Thompson would fast and pray with us.

So with family and friends fasting and praying with us from Saturday through Wednesday, we went back to the doctor's office on Thursday morning for another ultrasound. Oh! I wish you could have seen the look on the doctor's face as he said, "I don't believe this."

"What?" I asked.

"There's a good heartbeat and this baby has grown."

All I could do was stand, pump my arm into the air, and shout, "Thank you Jesus!" After shedding tears of joy and thanks, we had a little further conversation with the doctor. He said he could not explain medically what had happened. The results should have been the same. He left the room visibly shaken by the results of this test. His nurse returned to tell us we could leave, already well aware of what had just happened. By the time we left the room and went to check out, the entire office staff had heard and was in awe of this event.

On Monday, September 18, 2000, Aubriana was born, perfectly healthy and beautiful. Four years later Aubriana is a healthy, intelligent, energetic, beautiful, and much-loved little girl. To God be the glory!

Aubriana Gordon

21

Hadley Family Is Proof That Miracles Do Happen

by Dan & Marie Hadley

*D*o you believe in miracles? Do you think of your children as miracles? We do. Dan and I have three children, Jan, Kim, and Beth. We now also have five grandchildren. There are other types of miracles all about us; all we have to do is recognize them. I want to tell you about one of our miracles, our special child.

Howard Kimble Hadley (Kim) was born January 5, 1964, at Bacon Hospital in Loudon, Tennessee. When Kim was born, our doctor discovered that he was afflicted with spina bifida (open spine). Our doctor told us that he had a tumor on his spine.

She said that during her practice of medicine, she had only three other babies born with this problem. They had all died. Our doctor gave us little hope that our son would survive. But our God uses miracles.

For our miracle, He gave Kim strength and willpower in abundance. When Kim was only eighteen days old, he was operated on at the East Tennessee Children's Hospital in Knoxville for the removal of the tumor from his spine and to close the spinal column. After the operation, the surgeon told us that all went well for Kim's survival but that damage had been done. "Your son might never walk," he said.

Over the next five years, our son endured other operations. These operations were done at Vanderbilt Children's Hospital in Nashville. These operations were orthopedic procedures to correct problems with his legs and feet.

Then came a day I will never forget. Kim was standing in the middle of the floor, holding on to a chair. I was sitting on the couch.

Kim looked at me and smiled. He turned loose of the chair and, in a bolting swinging style, walked across the room to me. I fell to my knees, hugged him, cried, and said, "Thank You, God."

Kim loves sports. In grade school, he could walk with an awkward swinging gait. He was allowed to play T-ball, softball, basketball, and tag football, not due to his physical abilities but possibly due to his perseverance and guts along with the vision of the coaches and players on all these teams. They saw the value in this decision to give opportunity and hope to all.

When there is a weakness in our bodies' structural components, the weakness does not show up in its fullness until the load on the structural framework has increased.

This is what happened in Kim's case. As Kim grew, the weight of his upper torso was more than the structural elements of his spine could support without orthopedic strengthening. Kim had such an operation at

Vanderbilt when he was fourteen years old. The solution was to place a metal rod alongside his spine. The vertebrae of his spine were clamped to this rod to give him the needed support for his upper torso. As he gained this function, he lost the ability to walk unaided. Crutches were the answer.

Kim wanted to play football for Humboldt High, but this was impossible. The will and the guts were still there, but the body was not. Kim is a team player. He always was. He asked for and was given the job as the team statistician by coach Jack Cain. As such he was a member of a state championship squad.

Kim then turned to another sport—bowling, a sport he could take part in. One on one competition. He has been bowling for twenty-one years. He has won many tournaments and trophies. He carries an average of 190.

Kim has another hobby. He loves cars. Not just any car, but Ford Mustangs. Kim owns a 1965, a 1976, and a 1990 special edition Mustang. He competes with his cars in shows. His cars have won many trophies. Kim was our miracle. Now I want to tell you about Kim's miracle. Did I say miracle? I should have said miracles.

On May 24, 2000, Kim and his wife, Stacey, were blessed with the birth of twins, Amber Nicole and Alec Conner. God's miracles always lead to others, so now do you believe in miracles? I do. Thank you for taking your time to read about our miracles. Keep an eye out for miracles. They do happen.

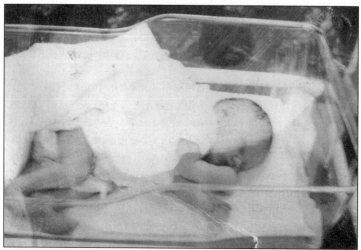

Howard Kimble Hadley, born 1964 with spina bifida

Howard Hadley, age 3 unable to
stand or walk

Howard Hadley walks with aid of crutches, 2004

God Still Answers Prayer

Howard Hadley's twins,
Amber & Alec

Howard Kimble Hadley family

126

22

God Answers Prayer in Mossy Grove

by Harold Jaco

*N*ovember in Tennessee is usually a pleasant time with frosty mornings and mild days. That had not been the case on Sunday, November 10, 2002, at the East Tennessee mountain hamlet of Mossy Grove, just forty miles west of Knoxville, Tennessee. It was a hot and humid day, almost as sultry as July or August.

On that Sunday evening, the congregation of about one hundred gathered in the beautiful new building, which was virtually debt free. Ten years of saving, sacrificing, donated labor and materials had produced this lovely steel building along the east side of U.S. Highway 27 in Morgan County, about nine miles south of the town of Wartburg, Tennessee. Pastor Anthony Pemberton and the members of the church were very thankful for what the Lord had given them.

The service began and the worship was getting under way. Suddenly one of the ushers burst into the sanctuary shouting, "Everyone get down and take cover! There's a tornado right across the highway!" By that time, the glass front doors of the building had been wrenched from their hinges and the building was trembling under the impact of that mammoth storm.

Pastor Pemberton had heard the storm coming and was concerned. He prayed, "Lord, lift the vortex of that tornado. Let it pass over the church!" Instead the Lord saw fit for that "black hole" of wind to slam into the building at a height of about fifteen feet off the parking lot.

The soundman for the church perched in a mezzanine-like platform off the second floor overlooking the sanctuary. The storm hit the corner of the building right behind him. As the fury of the storm broke wood framing, bent steel beams, and rolled back the steel to allow deluges of rain into the building, the soundman thought, "I'm a 'goner,' for sure." Later when he opened the thin hollow-core door, which miraculously had survived and protected him from the hand of death, he realized just how much the Lord had done for him. He walked out into the rain, stepping over the scattered splintered framing of the building where once had been a second-floor corridor and fellowship hall.

Meanwhile, in the sanctuary, the pastor had called for the people to come around the altar and join in prayer for their safety and for that of the community. As the building trembled and the ceiling tiles formed waves like the wind ripples a lake, the people cried out, some in faith, others in fear. The prayers and screams of the people were swallowed by the violent noise of the storm as it swept into the building and stripped off roofing, which allowed cascades of water to wash into the building.

Finally, when the high winds subsided, rain poured

down. The rain and debris, which came with the tornado, soon ruined the lovely edifice. All was dark except for the emergency lights, which had switched on when the power failed.

As the people went out to survey the damage, they walked into a war zone. The doors were gone from the front of the building. Debris was scattered everywhere. Cars and trucks were scattered all around. They couldn't see much, for all the lights were out in the community. Later they learned that the subdivision of houses and mobile homes directly across the highway from the church was a site of terrible destruction and chaos.

A quick assessment of the situation revealed the encouraging news that not one of the people huddled around that altar in the church that night had suffered even so much as a scratch. What a miracle!

The new day lighted the nightmare of what had actually happened to their community. Some of the people had gone home from church to discover that all there was left of their homes was wreckage and foundation blocks. Some of the families would surely have lost their lives had they not been at church.

Across the highway, the chaos was indescribable. An aerial photograph of the hillside across from the church showed endless debris and wreckage. Appliances, splintered lumber, brick and blocks, twisted automobiles, block foundations were all that was left of many families' dreams.

Later one lady said, "Yesterday we had a nice brick home and four vehicles. Today we don't own a toothbrush!" There was even a school bus lying on its side among the rubble. The tornado had actually stripped a path of blacktop from one of the streets in the subdivision. But most

129

sobering of all was the stark awareness that seven persons had lost their lives in the wrath of that vicious storm.

The beautiful new church building was a total shambles. The front wall of the building was canted possibly as much as twenty degrees inward. Large portions of the metal roofing was either torn off or twisted and mangled beyond repair. The metal sides of the building were caved in around the purlins of the side walls. The mighty main steel beams were twisted as though by the hands of a giant. Inside, pieces of furniture had been picked up on the entry level and hurled through walls of sheetrock in the upper corridor. Eventually the entire building had to be bulldozed, and a lovely new building once again stands on that same location.

The inspiration of Pastor Pemberton to call the people around the altar put them in the safest place in the building (but not according to conventional wisdom). The "experts" would have directed them to fill the hallways. But they were in the place of God's protection as they called out to Him for His deliverance in the awful terror of the tornado that night. They must have been dwelling in the "secret place of the most High," for there were no other safe places in Mossy Grove, Tennessee, on the night of November 10, 2002.

When God answers our prayers, He reserves the right to do it in His own way. If He had lifted the storm above the building, they would have been no safer than they were in His care as the building was wrecked all around them. We do not understand all the ways God does things; but we do understand that as in this case, and so often in other cases, the only way we can be protected is by the mighty hand of the Lord as an answer to our prayers!

Church before the storm

Church entrance and southwest corner after the storm

Church entrance after the storm

Southwest
corner of the
church

Right behind the
sound room door

Southwest corner of the
church

23

The Promise I Forgot

by Fred Kinzie

In the latter part of February 1980, Sister Kinzie and I returned home from El Salvador, Central America. We heard the disturbing news that the prime rate was so high it would possibly interfere with building our new church.

This caused me great concern. The rate had reached 15 percent and was still rising. What could we do? We could not pay such a high interest rate. We had money to start the building but would have to borrow soon. We could see no way to start the building on schedule. The architect's plans were finished and the construction manager was ready to go. But now uncertainty gripped our hearts. As pastor, I was reluctant to start building and perhaps not be able to finish.

I was greatly disturbed, actually fearful. The final word would be mine, and I was in no shape to say it. Should I call it off or postpone it indefinitely?

Rather than doing either, I called the church to prayer.

On a Friday evening, I went to our cottage in Michigan. I told my wife that I would not be back until I had an answer from the Lord, regardless of how long it took.

I was so troubled. I prayed that evening and finally retired without an answer. I tossed all night; first one thing and then another popped into my mind. Sleep was impossible. Troubled, I arose and began to earnestly pray. I didn't pray long until I heard, "Son, when have I ever let you down?" How and where it came from I don't know. I accepted it as from the Lord because of how it affected me.

Startled, my mind coursed back twenty-seven years to a prayer meeting in Orange, Texas, where God promised He would take care of us in Toledo. I thought of every crisis we faced financially. Ultimately everything worked out grand, often miraculously.

Frankly, I had forgotten His promise. Recognizing my faithlessness, I confessed my failure to believe. The Spirit of God swept over me, and I began weeping. I headed back to Toledo, weeping all the way. I told the church, "Let's go!"

It was scary for a while as we had to pay an outlandish interest rate for one month (22 percent), but it slowly came down, and we were on our way. The rest is history.

I'm sure that without that prayer meeting the result would have been, "No go." The building stands today as an answer to sincere and earnest prayer. Thank God for His faithfulness.

24

Visible Miracles
of Healings

by R. P. Kloepper

In almost sixty years of ministry, I have prayed
for many folks who needed healing. Our God
was merciful and kept His Word many times. The
place of prayer is not as important as faith—faith by the
one who prays and faith by the potential recipient.

God's power is not confined to the tabernacle but is
as mobile as our bodies, which are the temples of the
Holy Ghost. Through the years, I have experienced healing on the telephone, as well as in person, with the one
who needed healing.

I have not forgotten the title of this chapter, but first
let's look at healing as most of us experience it. Healing
involves a process of time that varies with the disease or
injury. When one experiences a flesh wound that requires
stitches, the doctor usually says, "Come back in seven to
ten days to have the stitches removed." However, every
second from the time of closing the wound, healing was
taking place. When it is a broken bone, especially when a
cast is involved, the instructions are, "Come back in four

to six weeks." Again, continuous healing is involved from the time the bones are set.

Most diseases in our bodies cause degeneration day by day, often at such a slow rate they are not detected until it is too late medically. I do believe that I, as well as you, have prayed for people who would have been called out of this world within a few days. Medical hope was gone. After prayer, there was no indication that a healing process had been set in motion, yet after a few weeks the sick one was out of the hospital and, a month later, back to work. What happened? Allow me to express it to you graphically as follows:

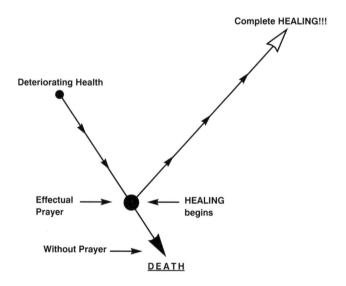

The descending line represents the period of deteriorating health whether a month, a year, or many years. The ascending line begins at the point where faith, with prayer, reached the HEALER and recovery began. The alternative is the bottom line.

The recovery rate can vary, but healing is not always evident even though it started at the moment of effectual prayer. After, say, three days, the person may be as sick as they were three days prior to the prayer but not as sick as they were at the time of prayer where the ascending line appears on the graph. Healing continues daily through the power of the One by whose stripes we are healed—Jesus, the Lord of lords.

I wanted you to have the background of the previous part of this chapter so you could appreciate my expansion on the title, "Visible Miracles."

Instant healings are miracles, yet they are not always visible, such as the healing of a defective heart valve, sclerosis of the liver, stomach ulcers, brain tumors, etc. To help build your faith for healing, I want to share with you several "visible" miracles that I have experienced.

I accepted my call to the ministry while serving as an officer in the Army Air Corps in World War II. My first ministry was at Fairbanks, Alaskan Territory. Civilian life in 1946 brought my family to DuQuoin, Illinois, where I served my ministerial internship and taught science in the local high school. Since I lived near the school, I came home for lunch at noon.

One noon hour, I found my wife, Betty, to be very sick with a "strep" throat. It was swollen even with her jaws and the air passage almost blocked on the inside. With a fifth-hour chemistry class coming up at 1:00 P.M., I must have prayed a prayer of desperation. I placed both hands around her throat and prayed in Jesus' name. Believe me when I tell you that instantly it was like squeezing air out of a balloon.

137

Her throat was without pain and back to normal both inside and outside. The fifth-hour chemistry class exam was given on schedule. This experience surely strengthened our family's faith in divine healing—an instant miracle.

Another visible healing was in the sixties during our pioneer days at the Tupelo Children's Mansion and concurrent pastorate at Cedar Grove in Tupelo, Mississippi. Our district superintendent, J. W. Anderson, had been hospitalized for some three weeks in an area hospital with excruciating back pain that required his use of crutches. He came to a service in our church where several ministers and the church prayed for his healing. It was another visible healing. He walked out of the church that night without using those crutches. What a miracle!

The next "visible" experience was an indirect report but was visible to our sister, Dorothy Rich, who had colon cancer, also to her husband, Brother Earl Rich, and later to her surgeon. The prayer was again at Cedar Grove in the sixties at the same altar. As we prayed, Sister Kloepper saw a ball of fire come vertically from the ceiling and pass through Sister Rich's body. This miracle happened on Sunday, but the evidence was not seen until two days later. The Riches, our dear friends from Illinois, returned home on Monday. On Tuesday she passed a black mass with tentacles around it; however, she still kept her appointment with her surgeon. After examining her, he asked, "What other surgeon operated on you?" Of course, she told him that she had not been to another doctor. He said, "There is a unique scar line where the cancer has been removed." Our HEALER had left His insignia for the surgeon as evidence of a visible miracle!

Now, for the most recent visible healing that transpired. It was my own experience at Cedar Grove on my eighty-fourth birthday, October 3, 2004. Our pastor, Brother Danny Robbins, was preaching on divine healing and stressing the point that it was necessary for the afflicted person to have faith.

For about a year or so now, my neck has gradually been curving forward and down. It was almost impossible to walk erect—my height was four inches below what it had been. Pastor Robbins asked those of us who needed healing and felt faith for it to come to the altar during preaching. I was the first to go to stand before the pulpit with hands raised as best I could. A tremendous shaking of the hands took place and then the freedom of movement of the neck came.

My former pastor in these semi-retirement years, Brother Cecil Greenway, said, "Brother Kloepper, I saw you getting taller." Others also observed the visible miracle in the congregation. What an experience! It has surely increased my faith when I pray for others in need of healing.

I'm believing and praying that those of you who have read my story of visible miracles will have an expanded faith for yourselves and for others for whom you might pray who also need a miracle.

P.S. May I remind you that fasting is a vital factor in seeing the impossible. RPK

Rev. R. P. Kloepper

25

You Don't Know the Way You Take, But I Know; Trust Me

by Henry D. McCrury

*I*n October of 1981, Sister McCrury and I met the missionary board of the United Pentecostal Church at their general conference and were re-appointed for service again in Indonesia. Immediately we began to make plans for at least one year of deputation for fund raising. While traveling through the Ontario District, Sister McCrury became ill and returned to Tennessee. She did not rejoin us until we were in the Connecticut District.

After the Tennessee District camp meeting in July of 1982, we returned to the eastern U.S. in North Carolina to begin deputation again. In North Carolina, my wife again became very ill and had to be taken to the emergency room of a hospital. Although she was very ill, I continued to travel and do the services alone.

During our travels in the district of Florida, we felt that our PIMs (fund promises) were coming in very slowly. I became a little discouraged. Voicing my feelings to Brother J. S. Leaman at headquarters, he tried to encourage me by saying that I was or seemed to be doing as well as anyone else.

Then we traveled to the Louisiana District. From the very first service, the Lord began to bless. We were so uplifted! We rejoiced that our PIMs were beginning to pick up. We shall never forget the kindness and support of the churches and pastors in that great district, as well as all the rest. We stayed in Louisiana for twenty-one days, and God inspired the people and pastors to give in excess of five hundred dollars in PIMs. I thought, "Lord, You really did know." However, this was the full extent and God was surely looking further down the road than we were allowed to see.

From the time we left the Tennessee District camp meeting, my wife would say to me, "I am so very tired. I have no energy." As is normal, I suppose, we rationalized and said, "You are just tired from so much traveling. Services every night. Several miles driving every day."

On Saturday night, August 28, we went north of Shreveport to Oil City to look for a friend and former classmate of our Bible school days. During our time of fellowship here, my wife again became very ill.

Sunday morning and evening, August 29, was our last day in Louisiana for deputation. Our morning appointment was in Shreveport, and the evening service was in Keithville, Louisiana. We were looking forward to the last service, after which we would head to West Texas for a few days of rest and reunion with the McCrury family.

The two services August 29 were greatly blessed of God. In the Sunday evening service, Brother Robin Boutlier opened the service, and the Spirit of God was mighty. After a beautiful worship service, the remainder of the time was given to us. Just as we began our program, a message in tongues and interpretation went forth. My wife and I both felt that the message was directed to us. The message was short and simple. "You don't know the way you take, but I know; trust Me."

The message was so powerful and so direct that I requested Brother Boutlier and the men of his church to gather around us, lay hands on us, and pray. I wanted to be sensitive to the will of God. Immediately I began to ponder this in my heart. Many times since that night, God has reminded us of the promise He gave. "I know; trust me." Many times I have gone back to that promise and reminded myself that He really does know.

At the time of that service, I did not understand the message to us. I thought perhaps we would have to choose another country as we were having difficulty getting an entry permit for Indonesia.

During our time in West Texas, my wife began having chills, low grade fevers, aching all through her body. We thought she probably had some type of virus or the flu. After Labor Day, we headed back to East Texas and the city of Dallas where we were to begin deputation again. On arrival in Dallas, we decided that she should return to Tennessee for a complete and thorough medical checkup.

On her entrance to the hospital in Tennessee, the doctor found that she had only half as much blood as she needed. This presented a different problem. Now we must find out what caused the loss of blood. After many tests, we received the news that my wife had colon cancer. Indeed the Lord knew that we didn't know where we were going because a detour to the hospital and major surgery were certainly not in our plans at all, especially for cancer.

A few days before her surgery, two of our wonderful ministers and their wives, Brother and Sister Denzil Richardson and Brother and Sister Darrell Pollock, came to the hospital to visit. One did not know the other was coming, but they arrived at the same time. This was the will and plan of God. As they began to pray, the peace of God settled into that room in the Jackson General Hospital, Jackson, Tennessee. Later during and after her surgery, others who came to minister, as well as the nurses, would remark, "There is such a peaceful atmosphere in this room." Indeed, God's Spirit was there!

The cancer had spread further than what had been thought. The doctor said, "I got all that could be seen with the natural eye." However, when the lab results came back, cancer clinically was found in seven of twenty-one lymph nodes that had been removed during the surgery. It had perforated the intestine wall. The doctor then recommended chemotherapy, saying, "It probably has already spread to other areas of the body." In a letter to another oncologist in Houston, Texas, my wife's doctor stated, "Without chemotherapy and radiation, this woman cannot live beyond five years." The chances of help in this were only minimal. The doctor told us that in 60 percent of all cases, the cancer would return; only 40 percent would not return. So standing on the promise, "I know; trust Me," we decided that with their 40 percent and God, that would give us 140 percent.

To most people, we were so foolish in our decision not to take the chemotherapy route. And to still consider going back to Indonesia was utterly and completely out of the question. At this time, there was not only one problem but two. Number one, the matter of a visa. It seemed that this was not to be. Then the matter of Sister McCrury's health. However, we continued to hold to the promise that "He knows."

In January of 1983, the doctor ran complete tests, then told us that he could find no evidence to indicate the further spread of cancer. Then he gave her a clean bill of health to return to Indonesia. In fact he said to us, "Why sit around and wait for something to happen?"

During this time, I felt strongly impressed to call Brother T. W. Barnes to pray. He is great man of faith and certainly in touch with God. Just a phone call was all that was needed. Brother Barnes explained to my wife that cancer was just like an open sore and that it would heal!

While we were in Houston, Texas, at the M. D. Anderson Cancer Center, the Texas Bible College, Brother and Sister J. R. Ensey, Life Tabernacle, Brother and Sister James Kilgore, Christian World Center, and Brother and Sister C. L. Dees all had special prayer for my wife's healing.

During this time, my wife and I were praying very much. One day in prayer, the Lord gave my wife a few scriptures found in Job 5:19 and 26. "He shall deliver thee in six troubles: yea, in seven there shall no evil touch thee. Thou shalt come to thy grave in a full age, like as a shock of corn cometh in his season." My wife has held on to these promises through the years.

For the next few months, we kept busy preaching weekends and revivals whenever the opportunity was presented. Finally, in the month of September 1983, our visa was granted and stamped into our passport before

General Conference in Louisville, Kentucky. After a lengthy delay from our original plans, we arrived back in Indonesia, November 10, 1983, for another term of service for the Lord.

We could never express our deep gratitude for all the prayers prayed for us during this time. We appreciate the kindness of Brother L. H. Benson, Tennessee District Superintendent, and all the local pastors of Tennessee, who invited us to minister in their churches, prayed for us, and encouraged us in every way.

Today it has been over twenty years, and we know that God has given us a wonderful miracle. Just as in the days of Joshua of old, the Lord said, "You have not been this way before," but we have the never failing promise that He knows, "not only where we are, but also where we are going." We must trust Him completely.

NOTE: The facts of this testimony can be checked at the Jackson General Hospital, Jackson, Tennessee, and the Jackson Clinic, Drs.

William Duval and George Thomas. The McCrurys have since served seventeen months on the island of Mauritius, preaching meetings on the island of Madagascar and serving two years in the nation of Ukraine, as well as building a church in Livingston, Tennessee, and pastoring there over five years. Bro. McCrury went to be with the Lord on February 25, 2005.

Rev. and Mrs. McCrury

146

26

Water for the Thirsty

by Scott T. McGarvey

*D*uring my tenure as yard boy for Apostolic Pentecostal Church in Moberly, Missouri, I have accumulated quite a repertoire of life-threatening stunts. The most memorable happened the first year we were in Moberly. The drought of the late '80s was in full swing, and the grounds were covered in weeds, grasshoppers, and choking dust.

One day as I puffed in circles around the backyard of the church, my throat parched and clothes filthy, I spied a spigot in the back wall of the church building. Immediately I found a detour to that spot. I leaped from my rumbling "steed" and twisted the handle of the spigot. To my dismay, barely a trickle fell into my trembling hands. Not one to be discouraged, I opened the faucet wide and waited while my cupped hands filled. The first taste was heavenly, even more refreshing than I imagined. When I had drunk my fill, I filled my hat and poured it over my head. Such a welcome relief!

So it began. Every time I mowed, I made pit stops at

my private oasis. There were times I even doused my mower to cool off the seat and steering wheel. The trickle never grew to the torrent I imagined, but it served its purpose well.

Near the end of the summer, a recent repenter announced his need of baptism, so Dad and I went over to check the baptismal tank. We eased the huge plywood cover back and gazed down into the water. An oily smear floated above spiders and crickets long drowned in a watery grave.

"Hmm, the water seems a bit low," my dad mused. Indeed, it was low. Nearly half the tank had been drained—in some mysterious way. I ran around back to my private oasis, as my mind raced, "Half a tank gone! All summer just a trickle. I'm feeling sick." I had found the headwaters to my lifeline!

"And if they drink any deadly thing, it shall not hurt them" (Mark 16:18).

27

"I Can't Breathe!"

by Vernon McGarvey

"Daddy, I can't breathe," was an oft-repeated plea for help that we heard from our four-year-old daughter, Jaime. She suffered from an asthmatic condition brought on by her allergic reaction to many things.

In November of 1983, Jaime's pediatrician, Dr. Clyde Gilless, arranged an appointment with Allergy Associates of Houston to have her tested to discover her allergies. After the testing, Dr. Leonard Hoffmang gave us a long list of foods and environmental items that were causing Jaime's reactions. He recommended a series of weekly injections to desensitize her to the allergies and prescribed other medications to be taken three times a day to cope with her illness.

Although we prayed for her healing daily and took her to the doctor for the weekly injections and prescriptions, it occurred to me one day that if God did not heal Jaime, she would always be sick from these allergies. The shots and medications just were not changing her condition.

Her medications only helped us to cope with the symptoms.

It became a regular routine for Jaime to wake in the early hours of the morning struggling to breathe. She would come into our bedroom crying, coughing, and asking for help. My wife and I would pray for her, but nothing changed. I confess that as a father, a believer, and an ordained minister of the gospel, I felt helpless, frustrated, and a failure because my prayers seemed to do less than the medicine.

Finally, in desperation, I would call Brother James Nichols, a minister who was a friend of our family, and ask him to pray for Jaime. Brother Nichols would always ask me to put the phone to Jaime's ear and place her Bible on her chest. Before he finished praying for Jaime, she was back to sleep. Jaime began asking to call Brother Nichols for prayer instead of me. It was embarrassing.

On a Sunday evening in June 1984, before church in the prayer room, Brother Nichols came to me and said that he believed the Lord was going to do something for Jaime that night. We went to where Jaime and my wife were in the prayer room and prayed together for her healing. It was a simple prayer, one that we had prayed many times. This time there was a witness in the Spirit. Jaime said she could feel something leaving her chest.

On the way home that Sunday night, Jaime asked me if she could have some milk when we got home. She believed that she was healed. I told her that we would believe God with her. Jaime had her milk and some cheese, some of her favorite forbidden foods that previously would have put her in the emergency room. So emphatically did she believe that she was healed that she would not even take her medicine that evening, and we believed with her.

She slept all night without a problem. That night was a miracle that has continued to this day. We never again needed the medicine nor any more allergy injections, and Jaime has never been sick with an allergy attack like that again.

Jaime, 1984 when sick

Jaime, 1985 after healing

28

A Soldier's Stories

by Lieutenant Colonel David McGee

Introduction

*T*he night of July 22, 2004, was a clear night with all of the stars twinkling in the night sky. The crickets and frogs were singing their night songs. I will never forget what I was doing at 10:00 P.M. on this night. What transpired at that point in time made me reflect over the last eighteen months and consider the many blessings of God.

I was walking across a parking lot, on a military base, carrying a message that was to be delivered to a family as quickly as possible. As I was walking, the slow, mournful notes of "Taps" began to play, signifying the end of another day. I stopped to listen to the song and tears began to sting my eyes. The message that I was carrying was going to be delivered to a family, telling them that their husband/son/father had been killed in action in Iraq. As I stood there in the parking lot listening to "Taps" and praying for the family, I thought back over the last eighteen months and counted my many blessings. There are many, but I would like to briefly tell you about two of them. The first blessing I will call "The Blessing of No Story." The second blessing I will call "God Is in Trouble."

The Blessing of No Story

On November 21, 2002, the construction engineer battalion (527th Engineer Battalion) that I am assigned to was notified that we were being mobilized to participate in Operation Enduring Freedom. On January 2, 2003, the battalion was mobilized and sent to Afghanistan. Before we deployed, I told the soldiers who would be stationed with me that we had three primary goals: 1) everyone to deploy overseas, 2) proudly complete our mission, 3) everyone to return home safely to our families. I went on to tell them that there were people around the world praying for their safety and a lot of focused prayers were being prayed for our safety. The 527th Engineer Battalion's mission was to provide construction support to the American forces throughout the country of Afghanistan. This mission involved the movement of over five hundred soldiers and equipment to two primary locations in Afghanistan. Once we were at these two locations, many of the soldiers would be moving to various Forward Operating Bases (FOBs) along the Pakistan border. The 527th Engineer Battalion would be responsible for improving the quality of life at the different locations by building showers, sleeping facilities, operation centers, and installing electricity. The unit also repaired runways at the airports and built protective barriers to protect the soldiers as well as equipment. A few of the soldiers supported mine clearing operations. Quite a few of the soldiers were involved in adopt-a-village programs and medical relief programs that required them to visit different villages. While the soldiers went about completing these missions, they had to keep their loaded weapons within arm's reach of them at all times. For the next seven months, the soldiers of the 527th Engineer Battalion shared this high-risk environment with thousands of great Americans.

I recall one particular event that let me know that God was in control and I had nothing to worry about. In February 2003, I was part of a twelve-man assessment team. Our mission was to collect information and make a recommendation on a location for a new Forward Operating Base. I remember calling my wife the night before we departed on the mission to let her know that I would not be able to contact her for a couple of days and would call as soon as I could. I knew that she and the rest of my family and friends would be praying. The team visited three different sites and collected information on potential runways, water sources, ground drainage, what construction effort would be required, what force protection effort would be required, and the attitude of the local villagers.

I remember the first site that we visited had an existing runway, so the helicopters landed halfway down the runway. As we were landing, we noticed a large group of people gathering at the end of the runway. Several members of the group had weapons clearly visible. When we landed, the team split up into three different groups and started collecting information. Part of our team consisted of a few civil affairs personnel, so their team approached the large group of people that had gathered at the end of the runway, to meet with the village elder. After a few minutes of meeting with them, our team members came back to the middle of the runway and informed us that the large group of people was upset about something, they were heavily armed, and we needed to hurry with our assessments. Needless to say we kept a close watch on the crowd as we collected our information.

I know of one engineer officer on the team who was praying. I'm sure there were several others doing likewise. Shortly after our team collected the information, the helicopters came back in and picked us up, and we continued on to the next two sites without further event.

That night when we arrived back at the base camp, we learned that several hours earlier two groups of locals were involved in a gun battle, with each other, at the first site we had visited. A couple of people had been killed. My mind went back to the irate groups that had gathered at the end of the runway. I believe that God's grace was the only thing that kept our team from being mixed up in the middle of this battle.

This is just one example of how God kept us safe during our deployment. Many of the soldiers were involved in rocket attacks while stationed at various FOBs, but none of the rockets found their mark. Some say that the enemy is not very accurate; I submit that God was (and is) watching over our soldiers.

In September 2003, the last of the 527th Engineer Battalion returned home from Afghanistan, and we had accomplished all three goals. Everyone deployed overseas, the soldiers accomplished hundreds of construction projects under adverse conditions, and then everyone returned home safely. When I think back to the memorial services that we had for ten different soldiers (from different units) who would not be returning home due to a helicopter crash and a couple of ambushes, I realize how great God's grace is to me. But for the grace of God, I could have been one of the ten. I have often had young people approach me, asking me to tell them a "story." This is often followed by the question "Did you see any action?" I'm quick to tell them that there is "no story." However, if you are interested in hearing how God protected a group of great American soldiers as they made great things happen, then I can talk to you for hours.

God Is in Trouble

On July 4, 2004, I asked my Sunday school class (eight-year-olds) to pray for my unit (527th Engineer Battalion). We would be starting our annual training on July 10, and there would be a lot of military convoys moving up and down the highways. There would be soldiers working with new equipment. The soldiers would be training many long hours in hot weather prior to the convoys moving to different locations around the state. I asked the class to pray for God's protection on all of my soldiers.

On July 15, 2004, I was sitting in the battalion operation center reviewing the training that had been accomplished during the first five days of our annual training when Sergeant Grant came running into my office breathlessly telling me that Captain Ayers needed me in a hurry. I could tell by Sergeant Grant's actions that something was wrong. Sergeant Grant finally caught her breath and relayed to me that there had been an accident. She said that Captain Ayers was at the intersection of Hwy 165 and 3130 and needed me there immediately. She didn't know any details, so I grabbed my sergeant major, and we jumped in the HUMVEE and took off to the scene of the accident. While we were on the way to the scene, a military police (MP) car passed us headed in the same direction. As the MP passed us, I knew that it was one of our trucks involved in the accident. Immediately I began praying.

The site at the scene when I arrived shocked me. One of our five-ton dump trucks had rolled and lay mangled with the blood-covered driver trapped in the driver's seat. The assistant driver was already in an ambulance. The emergency crew was using the "Jaws of Life" to cut the driver out of the truck. Other medical personnel were working to stabilize the driver. A deputy sheriff was guiding in the "Life Air" helicopter. Captain Ayers approached me and reported what had happened.

The driver had left the construction site with a load of wet debris in the truck and was headed to the dirt pit. When the truck got up around forty-five mph, the truck started shaking. The driver was young with very little experience operating a loaded dump truck. When the truck started shaking, the driver lost control and crossed one northbound lane, ran through the median, and crossed two southbound lanes. The truck flipped twice down the side embankment before coming to a stop. There was no other vehicle involved, and the injuries to the two soldiers were unknown. It did not look good. At that point, I did the only thing I knew to do. I called my wife and told her, "Call several people in the church and begin to pray." I watched and prayed as they put the injured soldier into the helicopter to take the drive to the hospital.

The sergeant major and I jumped into the truck and headed to the hospital. While I was on the way to the hospital, I called the battalion S-1 and told him to get the chaplain to meet us at the hospital. When I got there, the chaplain and I were allowed to go into the emergency rooms to visit with the soldiers. How it hurt me to see my soldiers lying there on the bed, strapped to a backboard, and covered with cuts! The chaplain and I prayed over each of them and asked God to heal each of them. The hours seemed to drag as we waited for results of x-rays and different tests. Finally the results came back. There were no broken bones and no internal injuries. Both soldiers were bruised, and the driver received stitches in a couple of cuts on her head. There was a time of rejoicing when we received this good news.

When we returned to the base and looked at the damaged truck, we realized just how big a miracle we had just witnessed. The cab over part of the dump bed had missed the driver's head by just a few inches. If it had bent a little further, the driver would have been killed. The next morning I learned that one of the soldiers who had gone to recover the wrecked truck found a copy of a sermon fifteen feet from the truck. The title of the sermon was "God Is in Trouble." The gist of the sermon was that in our troubles is where we will find God because it is during these times of trouble that we will see just how big God is and how much He loves us. Needless to say, the chaplain had some interesting material for his next few services, and there were a lot of thanksgiving prayers being said.

As I stood in the parking lot listening to the last few strands of "Taps" and reflected back on God's blessings, I was filled with many emotions. As the notes of "Taps" faded into the night air, the words of the song took on new meaning.

The day is done, gone the sun,
From the hills, from the lakes, from the sky.
All is well, safely rest, God is nigh.

God has shown me this last year just how great He really is and that He is there even in the midst of our troubles.

Lietenant Colonel McGee outside the compound signing "I love you" to his wife and girls.

The five-ton truck that was wrecked. Both the driver and passenger escaped with just cuts and bruises.

29

Two Women Dressed in White

by John & Nilah Mean

*I*n late July 1952, Brother Lewis DeMerchant and I landed in Stewiacke (an Indian name for "The Winding River"), a small town of about one thousand people, for the purpose of raising up our first church in the Province of Nova Scotia.

We brought with us, a mattress, a Coleman stove, also our necessary clothing and utensils for survival, plus a gospel tent on the back of Brother DeMerchant's half-ton Chevy pick-up.

Immediately we started knocking doors, asking and inquiring about a lot upon which we could erect our tent for services. It was but a few hours of this activity that our arch enemy got stirred and the harassment began with the shouting of hallelujah from across the street. This made us feel quite comfortable until the following words were uttered "Go back to New Brunswick, you New Brunswick bums." We continued for quite some time until it seemed that all doors were locked closed. Then we decided to go to a small town four miles to the south of

Stewiacke by the name of Schubenacadie (another Indian name meaning "the heading of the waters"). It looked as though we had two favorable leads for property upon which to place our tent. In late afternoon, this door also became tightly sealed.

We returned to Stewiacke and went down by the river, spread our blanket upon the grass, and called on the name of the Lord Jesus. "You sent us here. We have done all within our power to find that place where You would have us place the tent." We got up from prayer and started back into town. There was a man mowing his lawn. This looked like an ideal location so we approached him and made the proposition.

"No," he answered. "I don't want any gospel tent on my property." He turned and looked toward the ground and then offered, "There's a lot up on the other side of town that might allow you to place your tent."

We anxiously climbed back in the truck and headed to the other side of town, not knowing exactly where we were going. We saw a man trimming a hedge, so we stopped and presented our request to him. We were almost shocked, yet happily surprised when he answered, "Why, yes. The lot right over there is owned by my sister. Pitch your tent on it, and I will tell her." Brother DeMerchant answered by stating we would first go to his sister's house and pay her rent and get a receipt. We began ecstatically unloading the tent. We had it up as the sun was setting behind the western horizon.

We placed our mattress inside the tent upon a few boards on the ground. We crawled into our sleeping bags and went to sleep. I was startled by a loud shout from Brother DeMerchant, when I opened my eyes the tent was coming in upon us. Just a few pranksters. We got the ropes tied back and had a peaceful sleep the rest of the night.

The following day was filled with excitement. There were the advertisements to get out, both in the paper and radio spots, lumber to buy to build the seats for the tent, also the platform. We built the platform to open in the middle so as to have a place to store our mattress, stove, and extra clothing while the services were in progress. Then there was the piano to rent. You see we had already booked a very illustrious and capable evangelistic party to preach the first revival meetings, which would begin on the following Sunday.

The children of the community seemed to be very interested in what was going on, so we took an hour off from our working schedule to hold children's church. This proved to be very helpful in getting the meetings advertised.

We visited a corner store almost directly across from where our tent was pitched. Mr. Wilson Robinson, the owner was a very friendly man. In course of our conversation with him, he invited us to his home. This is what we were eagerly waiting for. So, we knocked on the door that very evening, Mr. Robinson was at the store, however, his wife answered the door. Her three daughters were also with her at that time. We noticed a very special difference between them and the other people of the town.

We were only about five minutes into our conversation when Mrs. Robinson made some remark about the blessed holy trinity. I answered by saying, "Of course, Mrs. Robinson, you understand there is no trinity."

With a look of both perplexity and surprise, she questioned, "No trinity? What do you mean?"

Needless to say, the one or two hours that followed were a most joyous experience. We learned that Sister Robinson, along with her three daughters, Juanita, Helen, and Esther had attended an old-fashioned revival crusade held by Fred Strickland, a hell-fire Nazarene evangelist. They were convicted of sin, went to the altar, and repented of their sins, and since there was no church in town that preached a message of conversion like this preacher. They walked with the Lord, holding services in their own home and endeavoring to project the Christian life even in their appearance with modest apparel.

Sister Esther had received visions from the Lord, which greatly encouraged the rest of the family. On one occasion, God gave Esther a vision of two women dressed in white coming to them and presenting to them the way more perfectly.

When Charlotte and Nilah, our evangelists, walked into the first service on Sunday night–believe me, they were taken by all the connecting events of her vision. Needless to say, these were some of our first converts in the Province of Nova Scotia. In six weeks of meetings, twenty-eight were baptized in the precious name of Jesus Christ, and God begin out-pouring His Holy Spirit.

It is also, worthy to mention that Esther later attended Bible school and married Harold Cole who is a very prominent leader in our works in Nova Scotia. Their twin sons are tremendous leaders among us. Jonathan is our district youth president, and James a very accomplished musician and a great leader in this ministry in our district.

God has raised up twenty churches in Nova Scotia since that experience. Seven of which the first revival meetings were preached by these two notable evangelists, dressed in white. To God be the glory!

Brother W. T. Stairs, the first Foreign Missions director of the United Pentecostal Church, Incorporated once made a statement, which incited in me a strong desire to fulfill our burden for apostolic revival in Nova Scotia. His statement was this: "It might be that our God will forgive us for not having taken the gospel to some remote village along the Amazon, but how could we stand before Him guiltless, if we don't share the glorious apostolic message with our neighboring province of Nova Scotia." Brother Stairs, in spite of his many responsibilities in Foreign Missions, was such a great help in both counseling and the many sacrifices he made to see the Jesus Name message proclaimed here.

After these many years, it is interesting to see the many villages along the Amazon that have heard the glorious gospel. Furthermore, we in Nova Scotia have had a part through our churches supporting our missionaries in those regions. To God be the glory that both the villages of the Amazon and the province of Nova Scotia have been introduced to the only saving name. Thank you, Jesus.

30

The Testimony of God's Power in the Life of Nathaniel Morales

by Nathaniel Morales

On September 25, 2001, I went about my usual routine then left to get some exercise. After finishing with my routine, I got to my four-wheeler to go back home. I was only fifteen at the time and impatient to get back home, so I was going rather fast! I came to a point on the road where another vehicle was coming toward me. We both could not fit on the road. I swerved to avoid a head-on collision but hit the back of a bus that was parked on the side of the road.

The helmet that I had on served its purpose to protect my head. That was a big factor in my still being alive, but the strap that kept the helmet on, fractured my larynx as a consequence of the impact. I was diagnosed with "Severe trauma to the neck." In order to save my life, an emergency tracheotomy had to be performed. The doctor said that I would have to have this tracheotomy for the rest of my life. He said that I would never be able to speak again because of the damage done to my vocal chords.

As the emergency operation to repair the damage

167

done to my throat and neck had to be performed, my parents were told that I had a ninety percent chance to live and that I would be placed in the intensive care unit immediately. After the operation, I was left with a permanent tracheotomy, and it took fourteen stitches to close the wound.

From the time that my parents found out about the accident and communicated to the elders of the church the need for prayer on my behalf, everyone began to pray and to intercede before God's throne. My mother said to me, "Nathaniel, we have a mighty God that is not going to let us down. There are many brethren praying insistently. Put yourself in God's hands and believe that He has everything under His control." After listening to my mother's words, I was able to place my trust in Him, and I accepted the tracheotomy.

I never had to go into the intensive care unit. Even though I spent three months without uttering a single word and had to write everything down, today I can say, "To God be the glory," because I am able to speak.

The tracheotomy that I was supposed to suffer with for the rest of my life was closed up after only six months had gone by. Here again was the hand of God at work. He answered all our prayers. God did not let us down. My God listened to my parents' prayers, and He honored their fidelity. My parents are very special to me and have been a very special blessing to my life.

I praise the name of Jesus and give glory to my God that makes the impossible, possible. I give all the glory and my everlasting gratefulness to my Lord. God answers prayer and is still working miracles in Puerto Rico.

Nathaniel Morales

Nathaniel Morales and family

Nathaniel Morales
Navy

Nathaniel on new motor

31

Read It Again

by Lois Anne Dyer-Newstrand

"ead it again!"

I did. He said, "Read it again! Read it again until you believe it!" I did. My husband, Pastor R. A. Newstrand, was referring to Psalm 91:10: "There shall no evil befall thee, neither shall any plague come nigh thy dwelling."

We were serving our first pastorate in Hartford City, Indiana. We had two young children, Timothy and Lisa, ages one and three. A "plague" of whooping cough swept through our neighborhood and our church.

Our children had not been immunized because we had been teaching at Apostolic Bible Institute, and one of the student family's sons had been given the series of shots and had tragically contracted encephalitis as a result. Consequently, he was in a near-vegetative state until his unfortunate death. We were all crushed!

So my husband made the decision that our children would not have the shots. I prayed! Then came the whooping cough scare!

171

Doubt swept over me like a blanket. Our children had been with others who were seriously ill (even in the hospital) with the disease. I was distraught, to say the least.

The children had fevers. I held one child, and my husband held the other in our living room of the apartment behind the church. He said that God would hear our prayer, and our children would not suffer this illness.

My husband had, and he has always had, great faith!

When he said, "Read Psalm 91:10," I read it once, and again, and again! I repeated it until I did absolutely believe it!

Shortly afterward, the children jumped down from our laps with the high fever completely gone. God heard and kept His promise in His Word. They never had whooping cough. It never came nigh our dwelling!

I have repeated that precious scripture time and again since that day!

God is faithful!

Timothy and Lisa Newstrand ages two and four, 1963.

172

32

Are Angels Real?

**by Kathy Patterson
as told by Pat McGaha**

One evening Melanie and Chip decided to travel to Ruston, Louisiana, to shop at Wal-Mart. When their shopping was finished, they loaded the bags in their truck, strapped their two-year-old daughter, Breanna, in her car seat behind the driver's seat, and then started home.

On the way home, Breanna said, "Mama, ant bite me." Melanie told her daughter that there were no ants in the truck to bite her. But again Breanna insisted, "Mama, ant bite me and it hurts." Melanie took her daughter's hand and rubbed it. Then the little girl fell asleep and slept for the rest of the ride home.

When they got home, they emptied their bags out of the truck. Chip went on into the house. Melanie went back to the truck to get her sleeping daughter. She reached across the seat to unfasten the straps on the car seat. As she did, she noticed a rope lying on the seat by the little girl. Suddenly the "rope" moved. Melanie screamed, grabbed her daughter, and ran into the house. She yelled to her husband, "There's a snake in the truck! Kill it!" Then she looked at her little girl's hand and discovered that there were two fang marks in the palm of her little hand. Chip ran to the truck and killed the snake. It was a copperhead! Melanie kept trying to wake the child but to no avail.

Immediately she called her dad, Rev. Robert McGaha, who is the pastor of the United Pentecostal Church in Homer, Louisiana. When Brother McGaha answered the phone, Melanie began to scream, "Daddy pray! Daddy pray!" When Brother McGaha found out what had happened, they all drove as fast as they could to the emergency room at Minden Medical Center. They prayed desperately every mile of the twenty or so miles to the hospital.

When they arrived at the emergency room, the child suddenly woke up. The doctor and medical staff immediately examined her but could find nothing wrong with her. The only evidence that she had been snake-bitten was the two fang marks still in the palm of her hand.

Later that night, after they got back home, Breanna asked Melanie to read her a story before they went to bed. Melanie took the storybook that the child had selected. It was one she had never read to Breanna before, a story from a set of inspirational children's books. Can you imagine how she felt when she turned it over to see the title, *Are Angels Real?*

On October 4, 2004, I phoned Brother McGaha's wife to confirm this story. She said that Breanna is the picture of health and was at that very moment trying to take the phone away from her grandmother. This testimony just goes to prove that Jesus meant what He said in Mark 16:18. "They shall take up serpents; and if they drink any deadly thing, it shall not hurt them; they shall lay hands on the sick, and they shall recover."

33

God Is Everything, Even a Handyman

by Carmen Quiles

t was the year 1965 and my husband who was in the navy was transferred from Pensacola to Jacksonville, Florida. He was given a thirty-day leave to find a house and settle his family. We found a house and a school for the children. We furnished the house and acquired the rest of the things that were necessary for housekeeping.

When the thirty days were up, my husband got up and went to work in the morning. But, at around ten o'clock that morning, he was back home again. I was surprised to see him home so early. He told me that he had orders to go to the Philippines the next day. I just couldn't believe it! I didn't know anybody yet and church people were new to me. What could I do? This is the way of the navy.

Since I don't drive, my husband went to the supermarket and bought a lot of groceries, meat, bread, etc. so our refrigerator and the freezer were packed to the hilt with food. The next day, he was deployed to the Philippine islands

Three days after he had left, I went to get something from the freezer and what do you know, everything was melting! I went to find the warranty papers to see if I could get the refrigerator fixed, but the warranty had expired two days prior to the refrigerator breaking down. I was so upset that I started to cry. I didn't know what to do, but I did know how to pray. And that's what I did. I placed my hands on the refrigerator, and I commanded it to begin working again and to start freezing again. Nothing happened. I went to my bedroom, dropped down on my knees, and prayed again. I went back to the kitchen and opened the door, but nothing was happening. Water was dripping down and out of the refrigerator because all the ice was melting. That was some experience! I laid my hands on it again and said, "In the name of Jesus, I need everything that is in this refrigerator for my children to eat. My husband is away, and I don't know anyone here who can help me."

While I was still praying, I heard the motor begin to run again! Praise God! It continued to work for the next two years when we no longer needed it and sold it. God answers any prayer!

Two weeks later, the whole plumbing system backed up, and there was water all over the place. By this time, I had met and was familiar with the neighbor in front of us, Mrs. Hall. In tears, I went over to her home and explained the situation. Mrs. Hall called a government agency and was told by them that if the problem was inside the house, I would have to pay one thousand dollars to have the plumbing repaired. If the problem was outside the home, they would fix it for free. I went home, and I prayed and prayed, saying that if the problem was inside the house for God to push it outside. I didn't have the money for repairs. When the men got to my house to work, they found that the line was backed up outside of my house. Once again God answered my prayers!

Sister Carmen Quiles leading song service

34

One Weekend in an AIMer's Life

by David & Lorraine Reynolds

I wrote to Brother Varnell right after I took early retirement, after serving thirty years in the public schools. I wanted to spend the rest of my life teaching for Jesus Christ. I mailed the letter on Thursday and received an answer back on Monday giving me three choices, one of which was Papua New Guinea.

We attended General Conference, still seeking direction from the Lord. At General Conference, Brother Billheimer, who had just spent two weeks in Papua New Guinea, came to me and told me it was God's will that we go there. I told Brother Varnell that we would go. February found Lorraine, our son Richie, and myself on the plane headed to Papua New Guinea.

Engine problems in New Zealand caused us to miss the airplane in Sydney. Brother and Sister Varnell were there to meet us in Port Moresby on their way back to the States. We could see them through the barricade, but it took so long to get through customs that the airline sold our ongoing tickets to the highlands. Brother Varnell and

Brother Dege, the national superintendent, went to fight for our tickets, and a near riot broke out at the ticket counter. Brother Dege grabbed us and hustled us to the plane—minus our baggage. I wore Brother Dege's clothes for the next week. Welcome to Papua New Guinea. We were the next ones in.

The church had split and one group had Brother Carver deported from the country. When Roscoe Seay came in with his wife (his "Sweet Thing"), he was soon beaten up and also sent out of the country. He turned around and came back in only to be arrested and permanently deported.

During the first night in the mission house all by ourselves, the alarm went off—and we did not know the cause or how to shut it off. The telephone had been shut off for lack of paying the bill and the electricity was about to go. The bank assured me that I could get money wired from the States—but it would take at least thirty days. The first Sunday we started out for church, with a group of young bodyguards walking with us.

Do you feel the call to be an AIMer?

Our real adventure began two weeks later when Brother Dege planned an evangelistic tour of three churches in a remote part of the country. He said there were no facilities for Lorraine, but he wanted Richie and me to go along and to minister. To get there, we started down the main road in the Sheaves for Christ vehicle heading to the coastal city of Lae. After driving for a little while, we came to a very windy road. Brother Dege began to speed. I asked him why. He told me that this was "Rascal" country. I asked him what was a "rascal"? He said they were robbers and that he had been robbed four times. He also said that missionaries had been stopped and stripped of all clothes and made to walk for help naked. This made me feel very uncomfortable.

I was much relieved to make it to the junction where we were to turn to go up in the hills where our churches were located. We came to a portion of the road that had some logs over a very deep gully. Richie and I got out and walked. Brother Dege got the SUV over the logs and around a washout; we then got back in the car. We arrived at a little native church just in time to put our things in a house belonging to a policeman. He allowed us to sleep there that night. The church was packed and the people worshiped God. I ministered and God moved, and a number received the Holy Ghost.

The next morning we packed to go on. Two young men came up with homemade shotguns. They looked crudely like guns, but the barrels were pipes just the size to hold a shell. The barrel was mounted in a crude stock and had a thick piece of rubber tubing, which one could pull back like a slingshot. When it was let go, it would hit a pin affair, which set off the shotgun shell. I asked Brother Dege, "Why are these men riding with us?"

"They are here to protect us," he answered.

"Do they have any shells?" I inquired.

"No, it is illegal to have ammunition," he replied.

The young men got in the back with Richie, and we started off. Along the way, Brother Dege suddenly said, "Do you see that gully over there?" I said that I did. He went on to explain that two weeks before, the "rascals" had stopped a missionary and demanded that he get out of the car. When he refused, they pushed the car over the side. I never did know what happened to the missionary.

After a couple of hours of travel, we came to a beautiful place. The scenery was gorgeous. Brother Dege parked the car, and we all unpacked. Out of nowhere came many young men who grabbed our baggage, including a generator and speaker system. They put all our equipment on their heads. We started down the gully and over a log across the river. The procession then began winding to the top of a very high hill. At the top was a level area where the tribes met to socialize and to choose wives. Around the enclosure were booths to sleep in. At one end, they had built a platform decorated with flowers for the service to be held that night.

People from four or five churches began to arrive. Each family brought yams, pumpkins, bananas, etc. and added them to the fire pit where they were cooking the food. When it was cooked, they placed it on banana leaves and allowed the people to come and to break off what they wanted. In the meantime, the dogs were walking around. I developed a preference for bananas in the skin, peanuts in the shell, and corn with the husk still on—I wonder why.

That evening we had a wonderful service. God moved in a mighty way. One of the highlights was that a church put on a drama of Jesus going to Calvary. The actor was dressed in nothing but a loincloth, carrying a cross. It took him twenty minutes to stumble the thirty feet to the platform wailing and weeping all the way as others were beating on him.

They were gracious and allowed Richie and me to put our sleeping bags on a bamboo sleeping shelf in the chief's house. I slept well but woke with about one hundred fleabites all over my body.

The next morning we all started down to the river for a baptismal service. The baptism was beautiful. Three elders were in the river baptizing over forty people. People were upstream throwing flower petals into the water to float down among the candidates.

After the baptism service, we loaded up the SUV and drove to another area. We parked and walked a trail up to a little village where they told me that we were the only white people who had ever been there. They called a short service, at which time about ten people wanted to be baptized. Brother Dege and I got into the most beautiful mountain stream just underneath a small waterfall where we each baptized five people in the wonderful name of Jesus. This was my first experience baptizing.

Now for the exciting part.

We loaded up and started for home. Everything was going just fine. We turned a corner, and two gunmen stepped out in front of the SUV and waved us down. I tried to get under the seat. Two more "rascals" stepped out with guns behind the vehicle. Two of the guns were within five feet and pointed at Richie's head. (Remember, I am under the floor mat). Brother Dege told me later that he does not know why he did it, but he put the vehicle into gear and took off uphill. This was the only time he had ever disobeyed them.

The next week, in the same spot, a truck driver was killed and his partner was put into the hospital.

Now for the rest of the story—Lorraine's.

My heart was full of thanksgiving for my husband and my son when they arrived home safely. While they were gone, I had a heavy burden and a feeling that I must fast and pray for them.

The burden did not lift until about three o'clock on Sunday—and I knew that they were all right. They arrived home about six o'clock that evening.

They brought a good report of the moving of God after the preaching of the Word. Forty-four were filled with the Holy Ghost, and they had baptized sixty-three in the name of Jesus.

When they told me their "rascal" story, I was glad that I had listened to God and prayed. After it was all over, we rejoiced greatly.

35

God's Generational
Faithfulness

by Ruth Rieder-Harvey

*T*he message of God's generational faithfulness is an underlying theme throughout Holy Writ. In Deuteronomy 7:9, the prophet Moses spoke of God's covenant mercy extended to those who love and obey Him unto a thousand generations. This descriptive dialogue encapsulates God's amazing ability to remain faithful throughout every succeeding generation.

Coming from a long line of apostolic ancestry, our family has time and again experienced God's generational faithfulness. Reaching into my treasure chest of precious memories, I would like to pull out a few stories which illustrate this profound principle of God's changeless character.

Many years ago, my grandfather, Rev. Andrew D. Urshan, was invited to minister at the Tennessee camp meeting along with his son, Rev. Nathaniel A. Urshan. While en route to these special services, Grandpa Urshan became extremely ill with a gallbladder attack. His illness necessitated an emergency landing of the plane he was traveling on along with immediate hospitalization. Meanwhile, Brother N. A. Urshan also became very sick and was unable to fulfill his ministerial duty for these meetings.

Upon hearing of his son's physical distress, A. D. Urshan summoned his daughter and son-in-law, Bill and Faith Schmidt, my mother and father. Instructing them to sign him out of the hospital, he proceeded to get out of bed and get dressed. Shaking from head to toe with weakness and suffering, this old pioneer of the faith refused to be deterred by the doctors or his family from his decision to go to the Tennessee camp meeting.

On the way to the campground, Grandpa Urshan said he was hungry and wanted a soft-boiled egg. My mother, Faith, reminded her father that there was blockage from his diseased gallbladder; however, his faith in God's power to heal remained unshaken. So, at his insistence, they stopped at a restaurant and Brother Andrew Urshan ate a soft-boiled egg along with a piece of toast. Continuing on to the meeting, he was constantly reaffirming his faith and trust in God's faithfulness.

By the time they arrived at their destination, the miraculous healing power of God had become operative on his behalf. Grandpa Urshan walked into that meeting totally healed by the power of God and never again suffered from gallbladder trouble throughout the remaining years of his life. When he came walking into the meeting, a man ran to the front of the tabernacle and was instantly filled with the Holy Ghost, speaking with other tongues. Spontaneous worship resounded throughout the old campground as the saints praised God for His divine intervention on the behalf of their beloved brother. Brother Urshan proceeded to have a prayer line to pray for everyone in the place. The shekinah glory of God filled the house as people were healed and filled with the gift of the Holy Ghost.

Grandpa Urshan's unshakeable faith in God released the divine healing power on his behalf, and his legacy of trust in God's generational faithfulness continued to live on in the life of his daughter, Faith (my mother), as illustrated in the following story:

On a snowy winter day, Mother was on her way to the grocery store. Slipping on a puddle of melted snow, she fell and broke the humerus bone in her left upper arm. Since this is the second largest bone in our bodies, that was tragic enough in itself. However, an even greater injury ensued when the fractured bone severed the radial nerve in Mom's left arm. Encased in a huge upper body cast, Mother faced very bleak prospects.

As an accomplished pianist who was privileged to study at Julliard School of Music, Mother found this was quite a trauma. Refusing to become embittered, she managed to take care of her five children. She also continued to labor alongside her pastor husband. Unable to play the piano, Mom opted to play the organ with her right hand and foot. Wow, what a legacy of consecration exhibited before us! We all knew where Mother's devotions lay— with the Lord!

During this time, many "Job's comforters" came her way. Even though they always seemed to know someone who had the same problem and never recovered, Mom continued in faith.

One night during midweek service, Mother was making some inner consecrations to the Lord. She told Him, "Lord, if I never clap my hands again, if I never experience the joy of playing skillfully on the piano, if I am unable to ever wave my arm in worship to You, I will not get bitter. But I will love You and praise You for the rest of my life."

About that time, an intercessory spirit of travail came upon Maude French, a little white-haired mother in Israel. The burden of prayer rested upon her so intensely that as she prayed, my mother thought to herself, "I know she is interceding for me. If only I had the faith to be healed." On that note, service ended, and we all went home.

Just in case the nerve should ever reconnect, Mother was wearing a brace, which held her crippled hand in place so it would not atrophy. The next morning, when removing her brace, she discovered that her left arm had been totally healed the previous night. Without realizing it, Mother had slept all night long with a miracle! In His own marvelous manner, God had worked yet another miracle for our family.

Overwhelmed with the magnitude of this miraculous occurrence, Dad called Dr. Eicher to report Mom's instantaneous healing. Mother's miracle was recorded in medical history at St. Vincent Hospital in Indianapolis, Indiana, and still stands in mute testament to the Creator's healing power.

This singular mishap precipitated many other catastrophic events. One event, which created yet another chance for God to display His continuing faithfulness, was my near death during this traumatic time in our family. When Mother was injured, I was just a seven-month-old infant who had not been weaned and was dependant upon her for my source of nourishment. Unfortunately, her injury disabled her to the point she could no longer nourish me in this fashion. Unable to find a suitable formula, I became very ill and dehydrated almost to the point of dying. Many times my sister, Beth, has recounted how awful it was to see me lying in the hospital almost totally lifeless. Yet, in the midst of their trials, my parents did not complain or charge God foolishly. On the contrary, they continued in faithful devotion to the Lord, and once again, His divine power was released on my behalf as He totally restored health to my little body. Glory to His name!

These magnificent manifestations of God's goodness have left lasting impressions on us and are a continual reminder of His generational faithfulness in our lives.

"For the LORD is good; his mercy is everlasting; and his truth endureth to all generations" (Psalm 100:5).

Rev. A. D. Urshan

Sister Faith Schmidt St. Clair

36

Heart's Desire

by Sonya Rose

Delight thyself also in the LORD; and he shall give thee the desires of thine heart (Psalm 37:4).

My husband and I have been blessed from the very beginning. We were both raised in strong, loving, religious families. I in an Apostolic Pentecostal one, and he in a Baptist one. We met in 1990, and he began coming to church with me. We dated for nearly three years before marrying in 1993. Our background is important, for it is the love and support of our families, both our biological one and church one, as well as, the faith in God that was instilled in both of us as young children that would carry us in the years to come.

In 1996 I was finishing college when I became pregnant with our first child. We had a plan on how our lives would go, but as it so often happens, God usually has a different one. Although there was no definite reason to

191

worry, throughout the entire pregnancy, I could not shake the feeling that something was not right. Montana Summer was born in late October and appeared completely healthy. However, even while still in the hospital with her, I was overcome with a sense that all was not right. This feeling increased as we took her home, and it became obvious that she was not a normal newborn. She rarely cried and would not eat. Each feeding would turn into hours of crying and pleading for her to eat just a small amount. Over the next few months, we endured weekly weigh-ins and changes in formula all to no avail. It also became apparent that she was missing developmental milestones and had weak muscle tone or was what doctors call a "floppy" baby. At six months, she contracted RSV, a respiratory infection, that landed her in the hospital. After this, breathing problems were common for her, and she was in and out of the hospital nearly every three months. At the age of one, she was finally diagnosed with a metabolic disorder known as Short Chain Acyl-CoA Dehydrogenase Disorder or SCAD. Basically, her body cannot break down fat completely. This explained why she could not gain weight, but not the breathing difficulties or the developmental delay or the severe scoliosis she now had. To this day, doctors have not been able to find an explanation for all the problems that makeup the complete package of Montana.

Personally, 1997 was a very difficult year for me. I felt as if I existed in some parallel world where my life had stalled, and I was standing still while everyone else went along their merry way. My husband was in denial about the whole problem. He is eternally optimistic and would always tell me that everything would be fine. I knew deep down this was not true. Since we were at opposite ends of the spectrum, we rarely talked about what needed to be talked about. Sort of like ignoring the elephant in the room. We learned through devastating trial and error to basically not take Montana anywhere. You never knew what was going to set her off into a breathing emergency. I learned to do the shopping when my husband came home from work, and we never went anywhere as a family. The one exception was church. However, I even had a tough time going there. My baby was not like all the other babies. She was scrawny and sickly and could barely even hold her head up despite being nearly a year old. It was hard to pray. It was even harder to trust God. My biggest fear at that point was losing her. I was also having trouble coming to terms with how my life was turning out. By this point in time, I had expected to be starting a career somewhere in the science community. Instead I was still working part-time at the retail store where I had worked all through high school and college. I've read that it's not the twists and turns life gives us that shock us. It is how much those detours differ from our expectations. Late in 1997, I began to work at our church, The World of Pentecost. This job was an answer to prayer. I was able to work part-time, and they were very understanding when I needed off to be with Montana.

The next couple of years were a roller coaster of good and bad times all revolving around Montana's health. Now they seem a blur of doctors visits, therapy sessions, and hospitalizations. In spring of 1998, she was given a gastrointestinal tube (g-tube) when it was discovered that she would aspirate a little bit each time she ate. In truth, this was a relief since it eliminated the anxiety-ridden feeding sessions we had endured each day. Now she was fed by a feeding pump. She did make great progress after this due to the fact she was getting her minimum nutritional requirements met for the first time in her life. She became stronger and somewhat healthier even learning to sit up on her own. I remember being so excited when she achieved this milestone even though at eighteen months she was a full year behind her peers. The g-tube wasn't the end of her weight problems, however. Again through trial and error, we discovered that Montana for whatever reason can just not tolerate a lot of food. To this day, she still only gets the bare minimum to reach her nutritional requirements for each day. Therefore, she still does not gain weight, and at the age of nearly nine, she is about the size of a small two-year-old.

By the time Montana was nearly three, her health had seemed to stabilize. She was crawling and trying to stand. My husband and I were dealing with the situation as best we could. We believed in God and that He knew what He was doing. Our marriage was strong, and I was learning to live with the fact that my daughter was different. I loved her just as she was. We then made the decision to have another child. Genetically, our chances were small that another child would be like Montana. From the first second I knew I was expecting, I prayed that this child would be healthy. I prayed that if that was not possible for God to take the pregnancy from me. About six weeks in, it became apparent that I was in danger of losing the pregnancy. At this time, I changed my prayer to asking God to help me sustain the pregnancy. I wanted this baby. You have to be careful how you pray because, after all, God does answer prayer. My pregnancy continued and all was well for the first four to five months. I even had several dreams where I saw myself with this absolutely gorgeous, brown headed baby boy. I was on cloud nine. I thought I would finally get to experience a few of the normal things about motherhood. Then one of our many ultrasounds showed us we were having a little girl. I was so upset. I cried all the way home telling my husband that this daughter of ours would not be the healthy child we envisioned. My dear husband, always the coolheaded and laid back one, pointed out that there was no proof or concrete reason for my being so upset. He reminded me that we were praying for a healthy child not a healthy boy. I told myself he was right and tried to push my anxious thoughts and feelings aside just as I had done with Montana's pregnancy. Instead of feeling joy and eager anticipation, I felt only apprehension and dread. My worst fears were realized at our next ultrasound when it showed our baby girl was not growing as she should. At this time, however, there was no other indication that there was anything else wrong so I was put on a higher calorie diet in hopes that would solve the problem.

Montana had been doing well but became sick around this time and landed in the hospital on her birthday. She was at the children's hospital in Indianapolis for nearly a week. On the morning she was to be discharged, I had a doctor's appointment at the hospital next to the children's hospital. When I arrived there, my doctor discovered that I was in the early stages of labor and unless steps were taken, would probably deliver the baby in the next few days. It was much too early especially for a small baby. I was to be kept in the hospital for an indefinite period of time. I just couldn't believe all that was happening. Montana was still ill, and here I was laid up unable to care for her. For the first time, I had to relinquish some control and let others take care of her. It was extremely difficult. I am a take-charge person. If I need something done, I would rather do it myself than rely on someone else. Now I was in a situation where I had to rely on others. In retrospect, this was good for me. It showed me that I did not have to do everything myself and that I could count on others.

I was in the hospital for several days on magnesium sulfate which, I have to say, is some of the nastiest stuff in the world. It was discovered during this hospital stay that the early labor was caused by an excess of amniotic fluid. The reason for the excess was unclear but most likely caused by some defect in the baby. I was sent home on complete bed rest and medication for the rest of my pregnancy. Mentally, I was numb. I tried not to dwell on the problems, just live day to day. Five days before Christmas in 1999, I was taken off my medicine and admitted to the hospital. After several hours in labor, events conspired in such a way that an emergency cesarean section was necessary. Both my life and my unborn daughter's were in jeopardy for several minutes. Upon waking from the delivery, the nurses brought me this tiny little baby lying in an incubator covered in tubes and wearing a yellow hat. I remember touching her foot and telling her I loved her before they took her to the children's hospital next door. Madison Winter weighed in at four pounds and seven ounces despite being a full-term baby. The next week was just a blur. For the couple of days following her birth, I was still hospitalized and was only able to see her once a day. This was incredibly hard for me. I am the type of mother that needs to be there with her child asking questions and taking care of her myself, and here I was not able to care for either of my girls. Montana was at home an hour away and Madison, although next door, might as well have been an hour away. I'm sure my husband felt just as ragged as I did. He was trying to work and keep things going at home for Montana all the while worried about me and our new daughter. He did an amazing job keeping up.

Once discharged I went home to see Montana whom I had not seen for nearly four days. After that, it was daily treks back to the hospital to stay with Madi all day. She was doing well. She was being fed through a tube down her nose (ng-tube) while they performed all kinds of tests on her. On Thursday, December 30, I was sitting by her bed alone at the hospital when this insipid doctor came in and asked to have a word with me. He took me to a small room down the hall where he proceeded to tell me my daughter had a disorder known as Miller-Dieker Syndrome. Furthermore, I was informed that one of the symptoms of the disorder was lissencephaly, meaning her brain was smooth. Whereas a normal brain has ridges and swirls, Madi's was smooth. He told me she would most likely die before the age of one, and she would basically be a vegetable for the time she was alive. I just sat there not really thinking. To this he added that she could stop breathing at any moment. It was almost as if he was trying to evoke some kind of emotion from me, but I had none left to give. Then he told me that he was going to go meet Madison! He had not even met her! He had only looked over some results in his lab. The emotion I began to feel was anger. I could not believe that this man could call himself a doctor and dole out horrible news to a mother without even seeing the patient he was discussing. We were discharged from the hospital the next day. It was almost as if they had given her a death sentence so there was no point in keeping her there. Again, we had tube feedings, medicine schedules, and doctors appointments galore. It would have been completely overwhelming, but thanks to Montana, we had been through all of this before.

Montana had recovered well from her last bout of sickness and was able to go to a special education preschool a few mornings a week. This was wonderful for her and for us. She made incredible progress and by the spring of 2000 was able to walk and say a couple of words. She and Madison were as different as night and day. Before Madison, I had only looked at Montana and seen what she couldn't do. Now I looked at her and was thankful for what she could do. Montana could walk and play and take some joy in the world around her. Madi could not. Montana could move and communicate in her own way. Madi could not. Madison was not sickly like Montana, and she gained weight with ease, but she was only minimally aware of her surroundings. On top of their physical differences, they were emotionally different too. Montana was and still is happy-go-lucky and funny and nutty. She is stubborn and difficult and a little bit mean. She can frustrate you one minute and make you laugh the next. She is full of vim and vigor and spite. Madi was always just sweet innocent and calm. My nickname for her was "Sweetness" because that was what she was. Although the doctors had told me not to expect Madison to do anything, I prayed they would be wrong.

They were. God gave me her smile. Madi's smile was something to behold. She had these big bright blue eyes, and when she smiled, they would sparkle. It was the most beautiful smile I had ever seen.

We had a special bond Madi and me. Montana has always been a daddy's girl through and through, but Madi was mine. She reserved her smile for me only. When she was six months old, she began having seizures. They robbed her of her beautiful smile and took away the one thing that had kept me going day after day. I was told that I would need to give her injections of steroids each day for the next three months to stop the seizures. I remember sitting in the hallway at the hospital crying and forgetting that she was in my arms. I remember thinking that there was no way that I could do this, but when I looked down at her, she was staring up at me as if to say I know you can do this and I trust you completely. I gave her the steroids which stopped her seizures, but they also made her bloated and uncomfortable. She was miserable and hated to even be touched. I tried to be strong, but I could see her failing right before my eyes.

Again it was a depressing time for me. I was not working at all now and spent all my time at home with two sick children. I felt like a complete failure, and I felt trapped. As a parent, you are supposed to protect your children and make their lives happy. I could do neither for my girls. I had no control over their illnesses or whether they even lived or died. Realizing this was a difficult lesson for me. Again I had to relinquish control to someone else—to God. I prayed for God to either heal Madison completely or take her. I couldn't stand seeing her that miserable. Again, He answered prayer, just not the answer I had hoped for.

Madison's body began to shut down in mid-September of 2000. She was put in our local hospital where I stayed by her bed around the clock. In the early morning hours of September 22, her vital signs began slowing down. I tried to ignore all the monitors as they were beeping and alarming telling me what was happening. I refused to believe it. I tried reading to no avail. I remember I was standing looking out the window at traffic as it passed by almost wishing it was one of those people instead of me. I looked back at my beautiful daughter. To my surprise, her eyes were open, and she was staring straight at me. In recent weeks, her eyes had gone from a bright sparkling blue to a dull grey, but at this moment, they were brilliant blue once more. It was painfully clear to me that she was telling me that she was done. All I could do was go to her and tell her okay. I called for my husband, family, and pastor to come. Madison was placed in my arms, and we rocked. I told her she was too good for this world and that she was going to a place where she would be whole. At a little past five in the morning on Friday, September 22, 2000, my "Sweetness" left me. That was the absolute worst day of my life. My most vivid memory is having to leave Madison there in that room and walking out with my dad carrying her empty car seat.

To say I was lost is a gross understatement. If I had not had Montana, I am sure I would have spiraled down into a deep depression. She was the reason to get out of bed in the morning. Ironic isn't it that just a couple years before she was the reason for my depression and now she was the reason for my hope. God works in mysterious ways. At the time though, I did not see this. I was hurt and angry. Emotionally spent. I could not understand why God would give me not one but two sick children and then take one back. It was not fair. I felt I was being punished for some unknown wrong. I did not know how I was supposed to continue. I knew logically that dying was a reprieve from a horrible existence for Madison, as well as, for me and my husband, but my heart was broken. I felt as if I would never know joy again. There was incredible pain not just over the loss of Madi but also because of the realization that we would never have a healthy child. Even though we loved our daughters immensely, being their parent was not much fun. It was kind of like a dark cloud that was always there. I hated passing the baby aisle in stores. Every time one of my friends would announce they were expecting, it was like a dagger in my heart. I was genuinely happy for them, but it was hard to see them as they went through their pregnancy all aglow with happiness and anticipation. It was even harder to watch their new infants grow and develop normally. My husband and I had obviously decided to not have any more children. We had brought two girls into this world with very different but equally devastating diseases. Why on earth would we chance it again? As time went on, I decided I had to reinvent myself if I was to be a good mom and wife.

In early 2001, I got a part-time job at Dow Agro-Sciences, an agricultural research firm in Indianapolis. I was a lowly research assistant, but I loved it. I was using my degree and working with people who had similar interests as mine. They were wonderfully flexible and understanding when I needed to miss work to stay home with Montana. In late 2002, we moved to a new home. I felt as if it was a new beginning. My husband's career was beginning to take off, and I was back in the work force too. It felt good, like we were finally getting our life on track and starting to live. When you watch your children struggle for the most basic necessities of life like breathing and eating, you learn to appreciate the small things. That's what I felt when we were starting to do for really the first time in our marriage. By Christmas 2002, Montana was six years old and had not been in the hospital for more than three years. A miracle. She and I were bonding like never before and being her mom was becoming more fulfilling, even fun. However, Christmas was always a difficult time for me, because she really didn't understand the holiday. She should be making out lists and helping decorate the house or bake cookies. On Christmas morning, I should have been awakened by two screaming girls jumping up and down on my bed in a rush to open presents. Instead, Madi was gone and Montana couldn't understand or participate in the festivities. Around the new year, I had a talk with myself. I told myself that I should count my blessings instead of grumbling about what I didn't have. Then and there I decided that I was going to be happy. I was going to be the best mom I could be to Montana. I was going to relish decorating my new home. I was going to enjoy my job and take it day by day. I was no longer going to sulk over not having a healthy baby. That was just going to be one thing I never had and that was okay. I could still lead a happy and successful life.

I kid you not when I tell you that a mere two weeks after having this discussion with myself, I discovered that I was expecting once again. I was absolutely horrified.

Immediately all the memories came flooding back of how awful Madison's pregnancy had been. I could not fathom having to go through something like that again nor could I face having another sick child. The wound that had started to heal was ripped open and hurt anew. I was utterly distraught. Once again, my husband's optimism and levelheadedness prevailed. He declared that we would pray anew. We would ask God for this to be the healthy child of our dreams or ask Him to take the pregnancy. This time I did not change my prayer.

My next obstacle was to find a doctor who would allow me to go on prayer. I wanted to be treated like any other woman who walked into the office and not a woman with such dire history. I found him through the recommendations of friends who were undergoing their own trials starting a family. The doctor was a man of strong faith who understood the power of prayer. He told me that if I wanted to put my pregnancy in God's hands than that is what we would do. So we did. What followed was an absolute miracle. I had a textbook, uneventful pregnancy. The entire time, I had incredible peace about the situation. As much as I had been certain about Montana and Madison not being okay when I was pregnant with them, I was now just as certain that this child would be fine. This time I had the joy and anticipation that I had so desperately wanted.

Our son, Aiden Seth was born on September 26, 2003 and weighed in at a very healthy nine pounds, ten ounces. He was everything I had prayed for. He cried loudly and ate greedily from the very beginning. The pediatrician that saw him in the hospital came into my room for mere seconds to tell me that he looked healthy and fine. I honestly did not know what to do. A doctor had really never said that to me about one of my kids. We got to bring him home immediately with no tubes, no medicines, and no future doctor appointments. I got to experience everything I had wanted. I enjoyed every second of the sleep deprived early months and reveled in how fast he grew. It seemed that I learned as he learned. I had never had to be a mother like this before. It was all so new and exciting. He is nearly two years old now, and there is at least one moment each day, when I still cannot believe he is mine. Here is the beautiful brown headed boy I dreamed about when I was pregnant with Madi. I believe God was showing me that I would get my heart's desire, but I just needed to walk through a few more valleys first.

I cannot describe the change that Aiden has made in our lives. Every day I watch in amazement as he learns something new. I still love to watch him eat. The first time I was able to take a cup and Cheerios to church for him, I cried. I had never been able to do that before. Small, simple things like that which most parents don't even think about as important is what I treasure. Before it seemed as if there was a running tab in my mind of things that I would never get to experience with my kids. Now suddenly I get to do each one. A whole new world has opened before me, and I could not be happier or more scared. It's a privilege but also a huge responsibility.

Aiden has healed so much of the hurt and heartache that we had experienced. We will always miss Madison. He does not replace her. We will always pray for God to completely heal Montana, but we have learned to accept her for who she is. She is everything that God made her to be. She still has ups and downs but definitely more good stretches than bad.

We have been abundantly blessed to know and love three extraordinary children. I am thankful for each one. They have each taught me something different. Montana has taught and still teaches me to be strong. She has been through so much and still keeps pressing on. It is a miracle that she is still here with us and is as healthy as she is. To look at her is to wonder how she survives. You just know it is God. Madison taught me to be calm, to love unconditionally, and to let God be in control. Aiden teaches me every day to enjoy that day. He has taught me to have fun, to laugh, to stop "sweating the small stuff." He has taught me there is nothing better than the love of a little boy.

I am thankful for the path we have traveled. How else would I know to enjoy where we are today? I give honor to our families who support us and help us in every way possible. I am thankful for our wonderful church family who brought meals every day when I was on bed rest with Madison, who never cease to pray for Montana, and who rejoice with us over Aiden. They have carried us with their prayers and love many times when we were too weak and tired to go on. I thank God that I have found doctors who believe in God's power. Obviously, we have not gone through these trials alone. We have had a lot of help. Most of all, I give glory to God for what He has brought us through and for not giving up on me when, at times, I wanted to quit. Through it all, my husband and I have gotten closer and are better people for it. We are just glad we don't have to go back but can go forward as our journey continues.

Madison Winter Rose, 3 months

Sonya, Phillip, Montana, and Aiden Rose

37

How Prayer Changed Sam Michaels

by Daniel Segraves

he real-life story of Sam Michaels came as a shock to me. After all, my impression of him was that of a faithful Christian who was always in every church service, at every prayer meeting, and praying with people around the altar area. Sam Michaels is not his real name, but that's what I will call him for the sake of privacy.

There would never have been a story told except for the fact that one evening the minister called him to the platform before the congregation and told how God had miraculously delivered him from an immoral life of homosexuality.

"Him?" I asked. "How could this be? He is such a wonderful example of a believer!" This testimony needed to be told to the world so that God's mighty power of deliverance could be witnessed.

It all began long ago, and that's where I will begin.

Even as a small child, Sam suffered deep emotional wounds, for he felt his father never really loved him.

Sam's father frequently abused him, verbally and physically. By the time he was fourteen, he found escape through alcohol and marijuana.

Sam married at the age of twenty and moved two thousand miles away from his hometown in Michigan. For a time, his marriage gave him much pleasure. Then due to the drug use, even this began to crumble. While in Texas, a daughter was born to the Michaels family. Wanting to be a good father, Sam sought freedom from drug addiction.

Within his own power, however, Sam couldn't stop using drugs, and his marriage became even more chaotic. Finally, his wife returned to her parents' home and took their daughter. Divorce proceedings began. The loss of his daughter and wife made living unbearable. Sam began snorting cocaine, and with this new addiction, his life took a steep plunge into greater sin and oppression.

Pornography became an obsession, and this led to the development of sexual perversions in his life. He began to hit the parties where people with bisexual lifestyles gathered to get high and to find sexual partners. The entanglement was like a web that pulled him into its hold, and he began a bisexual trend.

Sam decided to move to California to continue in his seemingly satisfying lifestyle. When he arrived, he met and married a woman who was a drug user. He wanted to break free of his bondage of drugs and have a family. But the pull of drugs held him tightly; he could not overcome them. His wife joined Sam in drug abuse.

During their first year together, his wife gave birth to a baby girl. Again he desperately wanted to break away from drugs and to change his life. He seemed to be a prisoner who would never escape the shackles that bound him. He began to smoke crack cocaine and to take crystal meth, causing him to deteriorate physically.

To support the use of these costly drugs, he became involved in petty crimes and spent time in jail. Over a period of two years, Sam served several sentences of thirty to sixty days each.

At one party, Sam and his friends were getting high on crack cocaine when suddenly he was overtaken with a sharp pain in his side and fell to the floor. No one seemed to notice, or maybe these so-called friends just didn't care. Sam seemed to be paralyzed on one side of his body. Unable to speak, he struggled to turn over to get someone's attention. No one responded. Afraid of legal ramifications should Sam die, his friends began to leave but not without taking his money first. They abandoned him to die alone.

Fortunately, they left the door ajar. A woman walking by happened to see him lying on the floor and called an ambulance. Sam had suffered a stroke. The next two months brought a stiffness and weakness on his right side. Gradually his strength and mobility returned.

Sam's wife was now carrying their second child. She didn't care whether or not their marriage survived, and she began to see another man.

Sam worked any side jobs he could get to make some money. A motel owner hired him. As they unloaded doors off a truck, the boss pushed three doors toward Sam. He caught the heavy load, but intense pain in his lower abdomen and groin caused him to fall under the load. Sam had been on a crack run for two weeks. That meant he had taken crack every day and had not eaten any food. This left him emaciated and very weak. The boss lifted the doors off him; slowly he walked the two blocks to his home.

Sam found his wife with another man, packing her things to leave. She was afraid Sam might cause trouble and called the police. She told them Sam had been abusing her. They arrested and jailed him. The guard frisked him, and this made Sam cry out in pain. Lifting Sam's shirt, the guard saw several large lumps or hernias protruding. They immediately took him to the nearest hospital emergency room.

While he was in the ER, a physician came to examine Sam. He told the nurse to prepare the other patient in the room for surgery, for Sam wasn't going to make it. Several hours later, the same physician saw Sam still alive and decided to perform an emergency surgery on him. He asked for a signature of consent, but Sam refused to sign.

The doctor studied Sam's face and asked him, "Do you have anyone you want to live for?"

This brought to mind the two daughters and the new child on the way. He agreed to sign the paper and went into surgery. He did not regain consciousness for the rest of the day. The next day, when he awoke, a guard was standing in uniform at the door. The physician who had done the surgery paid for the private room and did not charge any fees for the surgery. When he could be transferred, Sam was taken to the medical ward at the county jail, where he remained for the first thirty days of his sentence.

The recovery period during the first two weeks in the

medical ward of the jail was hindered due to his being malnourished and having drug withdrawal hallucinations. One of the medical staff taking care of Sam was an assistant pastor of an Apostolic church. He was concerned about Sam and prayed for him every day that the hallucinations would stop. He also read to him each day from a Bread of Life publication. Sam felt a hunger in his heart, and faith began to arise as he heard the Word of God.

After thirty days, he was transferred to the general population area of the jail to complete the rest of the forty-five-day sentence for spousal abuse. While there, an inmate told Sam he felt led by God to read the Gospel of John to him. The daily Bible reading continued. Some ministers visited the jail, and Sam learned of a Christian men's home, a group home, that he entered after being released. Over a six-month period there, he learned more about the Bible and receiving the gift of the Holy Ghost. After about three months in the home, he decided he would like to receive the Holy Ghost, so he went to the basement to pray. In just a short time, he began to speak in another language. He knew that the Holy Spirit had come upon him.

Across the street from the group home was a mission that was funded and managed by Christian Life Center in Stockton, California. It provided free food and clothing to anyone in need. Sam began to work there in exchange for food and clothing to be given to the Christian men's home.

One of the ministers at the mission taught Sam about the deity of Jesus Christ and the importance of baptism in His name. This caused Sam to search the Scriptures and study the Book of Acts. After completing the program at the Christian men's home, Sam began to attend Christian Life Center. In a short time, he was baptized in the name of Jesus. That was in 1993. He is still faithful to church.

Now a lay minister in the church, Sam works with new converts and teaches Bible studies to men and women in a drug and alcohol treatment center. He has been free of drug addiction and the oppression of Satan since the orderly prayed for him in the medical ward.

He looks back over the years with gratefulness for the miracles, blessings, and victories in his life. One of the greatest things to happen to him was gaining sole physical custody of his youngest daughters. Additionally, all three daughters have been baptized in Jesus' name and the two oldest have received the Holy Spirit.

Sam's oldest daughter, from his first marriage, came to live with him after graduating from high school. Shortly after her conversion, she began to attend Christian Life College and is now married to an Apostolic preacher.

One would have to know Sam Michaels to see the miracle prayer brought about. This is one life you really have to see to believe.

38

Changing God's Way

by Judy Segraves

While reflecting over the past several years, it dawned on me that something has happened in my life that is nothing short of a miracle. As I share this story, it might help you, the reader, to see that sometimes God wants to work in His own good time.

It all began in the year 1982. I was a typical pastor's wife. It seemed that I was involved in everything that happened at our church. There were Sunday school, choir, special music, tape ministry, bulletin mail-outs, hospital visitation, the Christian school that the church sponsored, bookkeeping, and even janitorial work to keep the church clean. There was so much to do. I felt needed and loved by the congregation.

Being the pastor's wife brought many unexpected events. Being a mother of two and caring for a pastor husband kept my life in a whirl. But I was content in the work of the ministry. Like probably all ministers' wives, I sometimes wondered if there wasn't an easier place to minister.

Then one day my husband got a call from the president of the very Bible college he had attended while in his youth.

"Brother Segraves, have you ever thought about being involved in Bible college work?" This was the question that began a series of troublesome times for me, especially when my husband responded with, "Well, yes, I have."

As time progressed through the summer, it became evident that a radical change would take place in our life. This was something I had not anticipated ever happening. I was going to be thrust into a position for which I felt entirely unprepared. My God-given talents surely couldn't include being the wife of a minister who was an administrator of a Bible college and who taught hour after hour. What would I do? What would be expected of me? My heart was heavy with a dark dread.

It was unsettling to move two thousand miles with two teens. A move and a new job should have been exciting to me, but they weren't. I felt very lost, even before we arrived at our new location.

We did find a home right away, and in a few days, the school term began. My husband spent many hours in preparation for classes and graded an endless stack of tests and papers.

At times I would visit the campus and wonder where I fit in. It seemed every need was already filled. I often felt sorry for myself because my husband was so caught up in the excitement of his new venture and I felt on the outside.

Many times in prayer, I would complain to God about how I felt so useless and out of my niche. Some thought I should teach college classes. That definitely was not in my inventory of talents.

One evening several months after we arrived, a missionary came to speak in the church that we were attending. He spoke and then asked the congregation to come forward for prayer. He began to sing:

I'll go where You want me to go, dear Lord,
O'er mountain, or plain, or sea;
I'll say what You want me to say, dear Lord,
I'll be what You want me to be.

I heard the words of the song; then tears began to course down my face. I couldn't sing. It seemed in the stillness of my heart, the Lord told me that everything was going to be all right, He would show me the way to finding my happy spirit again, and I would be fulfilled in this new ministry.

The cloud of darkness that always hovered overhead lifted day by day, and I began to see the possibilities around me.

First of all, my husband needed me to be a wife to him and to do all the necessary things a wife is supposed to do. My two children needed a mother to take care of their needs personally and for their church and school involvement. I saw places to fill in the church. There was Sunday school work. I joined the group who made food for families who were grieving over a loved one or were in a crisis situation. There was always a plea for those who would meet for prayer sessions.

At the college, I volunteered to work in the library a couple of mornings a week. The office often needed a fill-in if someone had to be away. When I was around the college students, I began to feel they were mine to take care of and encourage when they felt lonely or homesick.

The idea of ministering around a Bible college began to grow on me.

Now here I am, looking back over twenty-two years of being in this unique type of ministry with my husband. I have come to see how valuable this ministry is. Though the results are slow in coming, now I look on the fields all over the world and see pastors, missionaries, music ministers, educators, evangelists, and faithful laypeople who found direction for their life's work while in Bible college. Every year, a new group goes forth.

A good man's steps are ordered of the Lord, and if I had stood in the way, maybe many of the students from the past twenty-two years might not have been produced.

Judy Segraves

39

Kept By God's Amazing Grace

by Glen & Rachel Smith

We want to share our story with you of how God intervened and saved our lives while we traveled on I-55 North on November 3, 1991. Just the week before we had been honored with a large celebration of our fiftieth wedding anniversary at our home church, hosted by pastor Fred Foster, First United Pentecostal Church of West Monroe, Louisiana. This was also a celebration of our retirement after serving thirty-three and one-half years in missions, which included pioneering many of the Caribbean Islands' works and continuing in Central America and Mexico as regional director.

We felt deeply honored to have our director of Foreign Missions, Harry Scism, and our former General Superintendent of the UPCI, Stanley Chambers, along with several regional directors, Robert McFarland, E. L. Freeman, Paul Hughes, Lloyd Shirley, as well as pastors Robert McGaha and Charles Caldwell, all special friends who made remarks. Family members, Amy and Ernest Nunley, David Hall, Hazel Magee, stood in the ceremony.

My sister-in-law, Mary Hall, did an excellent job of arranging the program and decoration. Local pastors and other ministers formed an archway down the aisle with their Bibles for us to march under as a tribute of thanksgiving for their support and prayers while we served overseas in missions.

Then, just seven days later, on a clear Sunday morning after stopping overnight, eating breakfast, and filling up the tank of our 1985 Oldsmobile with gas in Sikeston, we headed toward Carlinsville, Illinois, to attend the annual School of Missions of the Foreign Missions Division. Glen Smith was scheduled to speak Monday morning during the devotion. We talked about enjoying the meeting, visiting with the officials, and hearing the exciting reports of the many missionaries. I had packed well, making sure not to leave anything at the motel, especially my 35mm Minolta camera that I had loaded with film and placed on the back seat to keep it safe and cool.

After asking God for His blessings and a safe trip, Glen set the speed on cruise at fifty-eight mph. We saw the open interstate highway ahead, no traffic in sight, so we relaxed to enjoy the beautiful Missouri scenery.

Suddenly everything came to an abrupt state of alarm. Glen was aware of the eighteen-wheeler topping the hill behind us, staying in our lane, but he thought surely the truck driver would move to pass our car. Then I heard my husband scream, "Oh, Jesus, help us!" We heard the crash as the bumper of the eighteen-wheeler plunged into our car. We were thrown about in our broken car seats, but seat belts held us secure. Glen's legs were pinned under the steering wheel. I struggled to reach for the steering wheel to help him, damaging my right elbow.

We were shocked to find ourselves airborne on the bumper of the eighteen-wheeler, which was pulling an extra trailer. We were told later that the tractor-trailers with their cargo exceeded eighty tons. For the next quarter of a mile, we prayed for God's mercy as we waited for the end. Surely, but for God's amazing grace, we could both have lost our lives or been crippled for life. Our car must have traveled two hundred yards hooked onto the front bumper of the truck before it finally stopped on the shoulder in the left lane.

Douglas Johnson, who was following behind the tractor-trailer, gave the following report: "I had been traveling northbound behind the tractor-trailer for a few miles prior to the accident and was on the interstate for five to six miles. When I came over the Blodgett overpass, I noticed the eighteen-wheeler about two hundred to three hundred yards in front of me. At this point, because of the size of the truck, I was not aware of the Smiths' car. The truck never changed lanes or weaved around. I did not see any other vehicles in the left lane. The truck did not try to pass the Smiths, and their car never was in the left lane."

He testified that he first became aware that something unusual was happening when he saw blue smoke and debris shoot out from the front sides of the truck. He thought the truck was having a front wheel blowout. The truck then careened to the left with our vehicle hung on the front bumper of the truck. At that point, Mr. Johnson was able to get a better view of the left side of the truck with the car hung on the truck.

After the accident, Mr. Johnson stopped on the right-hand shoulder of the highway, walked over to us, and asked, "Are you okay?" Then the driver of the eighteen-wheeler who admitted responsibility and said, "I am sorry," approached the three of us. "I didn't even see the Smiths' car."

Mr. Johnson opened the doors of our car, amazed that no windows were broken. Then he helped Glen out of the car. Trembling, Glen stood and laid his head on the roof of the car. The ambulance driver said he had expected to see bleeding, broken bodies, but he found only a totaled vehicle, broken luggage, and a smashed typewriter. Inside the ambulance, Glen was placed on oxygen, and his blood pressure measured 210 over 130, close to a major stroke.

When we arrived at the Delta Medical Center, we both were immediately checked and x-rayed. Glen had two ruptured discs. When we said we were Pentecostals, a nurse told me that their chaplain was one of our pastors. How grateful I was to be able to call Pastor Billy Butler and find out that Brother and Sister Stanley Chambers, the Missouri District Superintendent and his wife, were ministering in special services that very day. Within an hour, our room was filled with prayer and praise from our precious friends who had come immediately to be with us. Amazing grace, how sweet the presence of the Lord was to know He had spared our lives. We give Him glory for His divine intervention.

Monday after we were released, Brother Chambers drove us to purchase new luggage, and again we packed to leave for the School of Missions. How grateful we were for our wonderful friends who helped us. Brother and Sister Dorsey Burk, the executive assistants, drove us to Carlinsville. There I placed our exposed film of the accident in a shop. Thank God. He had given me presence of mind enough to think of taking pictures as a testimony.

The news of our accident had been announced ahead of our arrival, and many earnest prayers were made on our behalf. We surprised everyone by walking in, lifting our hearts and hands to the Lord for His divine deliverance. The pictures portrayed to everyone what a miracle God had delivered us with. It was a most horrible accident that certainly could have been fatal.

"Because of the LORD's great love we are not consumed, for his compassions never fail. They are new every morning; great is your faithfulness" (Lamentations 3:22-23, NIV).

Rev. Glen & Rachel Smith's 50th Wedding Anniversary, at First UPC, West Monroe, Louisiana

Driver of 18-wheeler said, "Sorry, I didn't see you."

Smith's vehicle after the accident

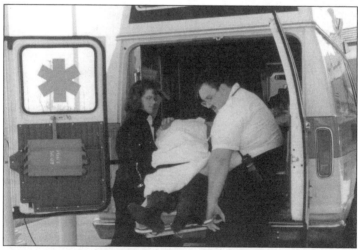

Glen Smith being placed in ambulance.

40

Prayers Answered Ahead of Time

by Martha B. Sparks

And it shall come to pass, that before they call, I will answer; and while they are yet speaking, I will hear (Isaiah 65:24).

This testimony focuses on an answer to a prayer that was not prayed and on God's ongoing provision before our need arises. If we follow Him, He goes before us; and everything we need is in place before it is needed.

They said the routine screening results were abnormal. I knew they were wrong but, of course, followed through with the recommended diagnostic tests and then a biopsy. My nurse practitioner, a longtime friend and colleague, met me at the radiology center on August 2, 2001. I had not asked her to come, but it was a comfort to have her there. She insisted on coming back the next day when they gave me the results. They were not wrong. I had cancer. Before I knew it, she had scheduled my appointment for August 6 with a young, capable surgeon who knew the most current techniques for my case. He was the son of her collaborating physician, and her call to his office set a smooth path for me.

The surgery was uneventful. I picked up the pathology report to take to the oncologist. As I read it, I knew my prognosis was very positive. The tumor was very small (14 x 10 x 9 mm), grade 2, and there was no lymph node involvement. I gave thanks.

My middle son, Randy, had a job that allowed him to accompany me to each initial doctor's visit and to be there for the surgery. I'm very independent and usually do things alone but wasn't sure that I'd be tracking well enough to process the information needed to make a treatment decision. I also wanted the children to have a part in and be comfortable with the decision. I saw two oncologists (one just returned from maternity leave the week of my appointment) and an oncology clinical nurse specialist (with whom I had worked for about two years). All were extremely knowledgeable and caring and concisely presented the information I needed. All gave the same recommendations for treatment, so the decision was easy. There would be four chemotherapy sessions, followed by radiation therapy, then oral medication for five years.

I was working full time and was primary caregiver for my husband (Bob) and father, both of whom had Alzheimer's disease. We had a wonderful caregiver who was in the home whenever I was gone. My youngest son, Rob, was also a willing and capable caregiver for "the guys." I worked in a city two and one-half hours from where we lived. My usual schedule was to travel on Monday to the city of employment and return home on Wednesday or Thursday. Most of my work could be done on any computer with Internet access.

In spring 2001, I had a grant approved and funded for the 2001-2002 school year. It included a work-study student ten hours a week. At the end of the summer session, one of my best students emailed and asked if I knew of a part-time position that she might be interested in. She accepted the work-study position and was a tremendous help to me in many ways. She capably completed everything I asked her to do and was available at the office when I could not be present.

I scheduled chemotherapy on Monday. Instead of driving to work, I drove to my sister's home. She and her husband had an upstairs area that overlooked the great room and had an office with computer; living area with couch, VCR, table, and adjoining bathroom; and a bedroom. My brother-in-law rearranged the furniture so everything I needed was very close to the bathroom. I could recline on the couch, listen to/watch gospel singing videos, or work on the computer and get to the bathroom with minimal effort if I needed to vomit. He also was thoughtful enough to place a pan by the couch.

I knew to expect symptoms to be worse with each treatment. The first session wasn't bad. I felt terrible but was able to go to work on Tuesday and continue normal activity, returning home on Thursday. "The guys" didn't know that anything was different. Their world remained the same as any other week.

The ladies of our church set a schedule to bring food to our home and provide general support. When they mentioned bringing food, I nearly gagged but realized that Daddy and Bob would need to eat normally, and I probably would not feel like cooking or be able to stay in the kitchen because of the food odors. Having the sisters come to our home was very therapeutic for me.

After the second treatment, I was able to meet my responsibilities but was so sick I knew I wouldn't complete therapy if the third time was equally bad. I prayed and asked the church to pray that it would be better. Our prayers were answered. I gave thanks, completed chemotherapy, and started radiation.

I knew what side effects to expect and decided I could handle them. God had given me two miracles, and I wouldn't ask for another. After about seven of forty-two treatments, my skin began to be red and irritated. Though radiation skin burns can be severe, I still determined not to ask God's intervention.

That evening after "the guys" were asleep, I was watching a gospel singing video. The videos were a blessing to me. I could rejoice, praise, or pray as I watched, and God's presence was so sweet. One of the songs was "God Will Make a Way." I knew He would. I knew He already had. At the conclusion of the song, the artist paraphrased Isaiah 43:2-4. "When you pass through the waters, I will be with you; and through the river, they shall not overflow you; when you walk through the fire, you shall not be burned because you are precious in my sight."

When she said, "When you walk through the fire, you shall not be burned," it seemed that God was extending His hand with healing in it, saying, "I know you didn't ask, but I see your need and am offering healing if you want it." Immediately I raised my hand and said, "I'll take it." The next morning the redness and irritation were gone. They did not return for the duration of treatment. Except for the mild dryness, there was no difference in my skin before and after the forty-two treatments.

God's answer to a prayer I had not prayed was very meaningful! It was not just the physical healing but also the assurance that He cares and extends compassion, when He could say, "If you are that independent and proud, you can live with the consequences of your choice."

In many ways, God answered before I called. Everything that I needed was in place before the time of need. Great is His faithfulness!

Sparks' family 1996, Kristi, Rusty, Randy, Bob, Martha, and Rob.

Sparks' family 2002, Kristi, Rob, Randy, & Kristi Sparks, Lawrence Brown (my father), Alex Sparks (granddaughter), and Martha. This is one of the last times I wore my wig.

41

Sometimes Answered Prayers Have Surprise Endings!

by Harriette Janita Sullivan

When I was fifteen years old, I was baptized and received the Holy Ghost. I attended a very small church with only a few dedicated young people. I had a very hard time getting to church on Sunday nights. The only way I could attend was to spend the night with my sister-in-law. This was before country homes had modern city conveniences. So on Monday morning, I had to get up in a cold house, wash in cold water, go to school without any breakfast at all, then walk about three miles to school. Now, if I stayed at home in my father's house, the house would be warm, there would be a nourishing breakfast, and I could ride to school in a warm car.

But church was such an exciting and vital part of my life that I chose to stay at my sister-in-law's home, in spite of the hardships staying there entailed. Attending church was like enjoying a part of heaven. What strength and blessing flowed into my heart! I was then able to face the temptations that were constantly bombarding me as a young person throughout the week.

When the weather was cold and snowy and rainy, I did not think of missing church. So I talked to the Lord about my situation. I prayed one cold afternoon as I was walking alone down the long hill from Franklin High School. Often I would use this time to talk to the Lord in my simple, sincere fashion. You see, Jesus knew my desire to go to church every time the doors opened in spite of the difficulties I had getting there. So I looked up to the heavens that day and uttered a simple, never-to-be-forgotten prayer.

"Lord," I said, "it is so difficult for me to get to go to church on Sunday nights. I wish you would send me a boyfriend who has a car. I don't care what kind of a car he has if he will just take me to church. I won't go anywhere but to church with him, and I will let my light shine."

I didn't worry. I just left the request in the Lord's hand. But would you believe, in about two weeks from that day, into our church came the nicest young man and his brother? They started coming to church regularly and began taking me home after each service. The car they had was a 1932 B Model Ford! It was a twelve-year-old car, but the upholstery was like new. The outside paint job was shiny, bright, and black. And I wish he had it today!

Then came an added surprise. After attending church for just three months, this young man was baptized in Jesus' name and later was filled with the Holy Ghost. He was as excited about his newfound joy as I was. In time, he felt the call to preach. We dated for about three and a half years; then he finally got the courage to ask me to marry him.

That is one thing I really prayed about. I knew that

marriage was for keeps, for my father had always told me, "If you make your bed hard, you will have to lay on it." Divorce was never an option! I prayed, "This is one thing in my life that I really want to get right, Jesus!"

The idea of marrying a preacher had always appealed to me. I had thought it would be exciting to be involved in the work of the Lord. It was, and it still is! We have now been married for fifty-five years. We evangelized for five years and had many glorious experiences. Later we established a church in Franklin, Tennessee, and stayed there for thirty years.

After we resigned in 1991, we became involved in the Associates in Missions work and went to Uruguay. There we visited twelve churches, and my husband used his master carpentry skills to add a small room to the home of one of the local pastors. He also worked on the head-quarters housing facilities. "Whatever your hands find to do, do it with all your might!" The next year, we spent four months in South Africa, where my husband, in addition to preaching, did some major repairs on the home of Sister Wilma Ruth Nix. He also helped to lay the foundation of her beautiful hexagon-shaped church in Mafikeng. What an experience! Things aren't completed as quickly in other countries as in the United States. We had wanted to accomplish more, but we did what we could with what we had in the time that we were there.

The next year, we spent a month in England and preached in several different churches in Liverpool, Sunderland, and Manchester. This was another time of blessing and rejoicing.

Then came our adventure to go to the Republic of Ireland, where we felt the divine hand of the Master's leading as we stepped out by faith although we did not know one soul in the country. We were blessed to see the hand of the Lord in providing a place for us to live and in meeting people who have become our friends, with whom we have shared the truth of Jesus' name. Some of them have even visited us in our home in the States! We still keep in touch with these people. We feel that there will be fruit to come as a result of our ministering there.

We also became involved in the work of Northern Ireland, where Brother Terry McFarland has built a fine church today. My husband helped to turn a barn into a nice sanctuary as a starter. Later we went back and helped remodel a storefront at a new location. Again, we returned when the McFarlands purchased three acres of land and a thirty-by-one-hundred-foot building. My husband helped to remodel the lovely chapel plus living quarters for the McFarland family.

When we first went to Ireland, there were no United Pentecostal churches in that country. Although we were alone the first year, we did not feel alone. We lifted our burden daily to the Lord to send reinforcements. We believed and knew in our hearts that God heard our prayers.

My husband was praying in Enniscorthy, Ireland, while the United Pentecostal Church conference was taking place in the States. At that time, Brother McFarland felt an urgent tug to come to Ireland. The Lord reminded my husband later that this was an answer to his prayer. Now there are several churches and preaching points. Little flames are beginning to ignite in various places with the beautiful message of Jesus' name. We like to feel that we played a small part in helping to fan the flame.

We have had a most wonderful, rewarding life in the service of the Master for over fifty-five years. If I had my life to go over, would I still want to marry a preacher? Indeed I would! The Lord has blessed me beyond my wildest dreams. We learned to put the Lord first, and He has given us many rich rewards! Blessed be His name!

Little did I know, when I prayed that simple prayer as a young girl of fifteen, that the results would be so wonderful and rewarding. Thank You, Lord, that You put that simple prayer in my heart that day. And to think what I would have missed if I hadn't prayed! Don't you agree that prayer had a most unexpected ending? After all, I wasn't asking for a husband; I had only asked for a way to go to church. But as always, Jesus gives one much more than one's wildest dreams can imagine! That's just His way of showing us how much He really loves us and looks out for us. How can I ever praise Him for all His benefits? So I will continue to knock on the Master's door. One never knows what new surprise He may have the next time I call!

42

An Unfulfilled Dream
Made Possible

by Harriette Janita Sullivan

I had always wanted to be a teacher. Perhaps it was an inborn desire. I had two sisters, a brother, and two sisters-in-law who were teachers. One might say that teaching just ran in my family. My husband and I often talked about my dream. All I could see were the obstacles. I was then thirty-three years old. I had been out of high school for fourteen years. We had four children, ages eight, seven, five, and three. I was a homemaker, a pastor's wife, a Sunday school teacher, and the church pianist! Enough hats to wear! But I wanted to become a teacher!

"Why don't you go to college?" my husband suggested one evening as we were discussing my desire to go to school to become a teacher.

"What? On a hundred dollars a week? There is no way!" I answered. Often I would tell the Lord, "Oh, I wish I had gone to college before I married. Is there any way?" I never seemed to get an answer. But on this particular night after my husband's insistence that I could go, I went to bed and had an unusual dream. I dreamed that if I talked to my former English teacher, Mrs. John Henderson, she could direct me and that I might be able to get a scholarship. Usually I am not one to go on dreams, but being a person of prayer and faith, I wondered about this dream.

When I got out of bed the next morning, I told my husband, "Honey, I had the strangest dream last night."

He answered excitedly, "I want you to act on that dream."

That same day, although somewhat apprehensively, I called Mrs. Henderson. She told me to call the superintendent of the Williamson County schools and talk to Mr. W. C. Yates. "He will tell you where to go to get a scholarship." So I called Mr. Yates. He was my principal when I was in high school, and he knew my family. He instructed me to go to George Peabody College for Teachers and ask for Dr. J. E. Windrow, who was the director of the scholarship program. He said for me to tell Dr. Windrow, "Mr. Yates sent me to see you." I called the school and was given an appointment. I was very excited! "Lord, are You going to make a way for me to at last become a teacher?"

Dr. Windrow was so gracious. He asked me many questions. What subjects did I take in school? Happily, I had taken college preparatory courses. What kind of grades did I make? I was above average. Did I know anyone who graduated from George Peabody College? My brother, Carl Smithson, and my sister, Sue Garlin. He laughed and said, "Why, I know them both. They were very fine students." And I found out that he also was from Williamson County! Glory be! I was in his office about ten minutes and came out with a scholarship! I promised to start in the January semester in 1963. Imagine that! A mother of four and I was on my way to college! I was so happy and excited that I did not think of the obstacles any more. I figured that if I got money for books and my tuition paid, the Lord would surely help us to do the rest.

The first thing I did was to get a *Harbrace College Handbook* on English, and I literally devoured that book from cover to cover. I wanted to be able to write correctly when I went to college. Mrs. Henderson so graciously tutored me on rules that I did not understand. How grateful I was to those who encouraged me and gave of their valuable time to help me succeed.

When January came, we had made arrangements for a baby-sitter for the price of fifteen dollars a week. We budgeted our groceries for twenty-five dollars a week. We paid our church tithes of ten dollars a week. We would pay our electric bill, water bill, telephone bill, car note, and house note all on one hundred dollars a week!

Mercifully, my sister lost weight and she gave me her old clothes. They just fit me. I was outfitted for college, and I didn't look too bad! I wondered, did the Lord let her lose weight so I could have some clothes to wear? My older son, Jim, got hand-me-downs from two cousins older than he. My second son, Mark, inherited my first son's clothes as he outgrew them. A lady up the street sewed beautifully, and she sold me eight or nine dresses, for eight to ten dollars, each season for Susan. The younger daughter, Anita, was able to wear the dresses Susan could not wear any more. We were all so grateful for our wardrobes. I finished four years of college in three years by going during summers. During those three years, we did not buy one washcloth, sheet, towel, or anything for our house. The last quarter of school, I did manage to buy a dress for four dollars to go to an interview for a job.

My husband and I worked together to get the children ready for each day. Then he would drop me off at school as he went to work each morning. He would pick me up as he returned home in the evening. I did all of my studying at school in order to give the children all of my attention when I arrived home. Saturday was washing, ironing, and cleaning day; never once did I miss church during those three years. We felt that the Lord's work was first and that Jesus would make a way for all the rest to be accomplished. During this time, we were able to keep our bills paid on time. If we needed a little extra, the Lord would send my husband a side job to help supply the need. And I was able to graduate with a 3.5 average. I'm not smart, but I learned how to study. If George Peabody College for Teachers could give me a college education, I wasn't about to let the opportunity slip and not show my gratitude for their gift to me.

This was the most beautiful experience we had in our married life. We learned to work, to share, to trust, to pray, and to believe that the Lord would help us to attain our goals. We learned to be grateful and to appreciate every blessing that came our way. We marveled that we could go so far on so little. My sister, Sue, would often remark, "Janita, I don't understand how you can make a dollar go so far!" I would smile and think quietly, "Thank You, Jesus. You still make a way where there seems to be no way."

I graduated in 1966, thirty-eight years ago. I taught school for twenty-three and one-half years at Cole Elementary School in Davidson County, Tennessee. Those were very rewarding years. One might say I was in love with my profession. I thoroughly enjoyed my work. It was a challenging job, but it was fun to me. How blessed I was to have a job that made me feel I had made the right choice. I have taught many first-grade children and have seen smiles on many faces as they succeeded in doing their work well. They were proud of their accomplishments.

God answered my prayers, and my dream had come true!

Cletus and Janita Sullivan

43

The Miracle Baby

by Terry & Tammy Taylor

had a great pregnancy, meaning I felt fine. No sickness. I had more energy, was happy, just felt great. I was about five months pregnant with my first child. My husband and I were so excited. Our baby was going to be a little boy, so we named him Travis.

On Thursday, August 6, 1992, I left work early. "I feel like I have the blahs!" I tried to explain. My monthly checkup with my OB/GYN doctor was that Friday, so I thought, "I'll just tell her how I feel."

When I went to her office, I told her about my feelings. She checked the baby's heartbeat, then told me, "You have the flu." She did not check anything else. She never realized that I was actually in labor. So I went home.

We were in the process of buying our first house. On that Saturday, we went to look at furniture. It seemed like every piece of furniture that we passed, I would have to sit down. I felt exhausted. No energy. Finally we just went back home because I felt so bad.

I called the doctor's office but had to talk to one of

my doctor's colleagues because my doctor went on vacation on Friday afternoon. That doctor told me that I would be okay. "But if it gets any worse, call back." About a half hour later, I called back and told her, "I feel much worse."

"Go to the hospital to get checked out. We need to be sure that everything is okay," the doctor advised.

We lived about forty-five minutes from the hospital. So we got in the car, my sister following us in her car as we raced to the hospital. About halfway there I started cramping badly. I began to cry. Finally we made it to the hospital emergency room. They put me in a wheelchair and rushed me to the neonatal floor. My husband had to stay downstairs to fill out all the paperwork.

As soon as I got in my room, they started hooking me up to machines and asking me questions. Everything was like a big blur because it was all going so fast. Suddenly I heard someone say, "You're in labor, and it's too late to stop it because you're fully dilated!" I thought, "No way!" I had never heard of anyone going into labor so early before.

My husband walked in the room as they were giving me an epidural. He only got to stay in the room with me for a few minutes. Then they made him leave because the room was so full of doctors and nurses. He was very upset because he had to leave the room.

As soon as they rolled me over from the epidural, the doctor broke my water. As he turned around to put the instruments down, the baby started coming. Since I was only twenty-four weeks, the baby had not turned around yet, so he was born breech. This was good because when his head came out and hit the bed, the doctor had not yet turned around. Had his head came out first and hit the bed, there could have been a lot of damage. The baby was born in fourteen minutes after I got to the hospital. I was definitely not exaggerating when I said, "Everything is happening so fast!"

Travis was born on August 8, 1992, weighing 1 pound, 14 ounces, and was 14 inches long. It was the scariest time in our lives. We did not know whether he would live or not. After he was born, they put him in an incubator and left the room. They took him to the NICU (Neonatal Intensive Care Unit). We finally were able to go to see him after a couple of hours. That was partly because they were hooking him up to all the machines and partly because I couldn't walk, for it all happened so fast the epidural didn't kick in until after the baby was born.

After scrubbing up and putting on gowns and masks, we were able to sit on stools by his incubator. It was so hard. We couldn't hold or touch him because his skin was so thin it would tear. But they really encouraged us to talk to him. So we did . . . a lot. The doctors gave him a 50/50 chance of living.

Later that evening, pastor Ron Becton and assistant pastor Mike Rickenbaker came to the NICU to pray for Travis and our family. They said it was so hard because they didn't know where to touch him. Travis was tiny, about the size of my husband's hand. The NICU gave us a lot of books to read about premature babies and what to expect. The more I read, the more I didn't quite understand. The books said that white males have the least expectancy to live. That really scared us. But the books also said to expect this or expect that, and he was doing so much better than what the books said to expect.

It is amazing what prayers can do! There were so many people praying that we truly believe that the prayers saved his life. God is great! They slowly weaned Travis off this machine, then that machine, until all he had to have was oxygen because his lungs were not developed all the way. We are so blessed that he did not have any major health problems from being premature, like so many unfortunately have. Travis stayed in the hospital for two and a half months. After the doctors knew for sure that everything would be okay and he was fine, they told us then the truth. They did not expect Travis to live. It was a miracle! They even admitted it. Travis was a miracle baby.

Today Travis is a healthy, active twelve-year-old in the seventh grade. He likes to do what any other boy his age likes to do. He loves sports. He plays football, baseball, and basketball. He likes to skateboard and is learning to play the guitar and drums. By looking at him today, you would never know that he was a preemie. Yes, Travis is a miracle . . . our very own little miracle.

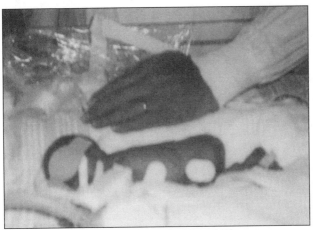

Travis, August 1992, 1 lb. 14 oz, 14" long

Travis, August 2004

44

A Miracle

by Angie Thacker

ooking back, now it is so easy to see God's hand in everything that has taken place in our lives since last October. Nothing happened as we expected but turned out to be a bigger miracle than we ever could have imagined. About seventeen weeks into my pregnancy, during a routine ultrasound, we were excited to hear that we were going to have a baby boy. Just minutes after finding out, our excitement quickly turned to worry as the nurse explained she had some concerns with the ultrasound. My OB, Dr. Branson, began to explain that his cerebellum, the portion of the brain that controls the central nervous system was either abnormally small or not present at all. This being the case he could die shortly after birth or be in a vegetative state for the rest of his life. As you can imagine, this was quite a shock to us both. He suggested that we visit a preinatal specialist at St. Johns hospital. The soonest appointment we could get was not for two weeks.

The ride home that afternoon was very overwhelming. We both had several questions and concerns. It is hard to admit now, but God was the last thing on my mind at this point. That evening after many tears, I finally remembered that I did have God to turn to. I remember just praying a simple prayer letting God know that I trusted Him no matter what, and I asked for strength for Dan and me. I immediately began to feel an assurance and strength that everything would be okay. That next week, Dan asked me to pray that God would give him the same faith that I was feeling. I did and the next day he came home from work and let me know that he too was feeling strength and faith that everything was going to work out.

Over the next couple weeks, it seemed like every message Brother Tracy preached was on faith. We also had a miracle service with Brother Rudy Theissen. Dan and I had been praying leading up to the miracle service that God would heal our baby completely, and it would be a testimony for the doctor's and specialists. Brother Theissen prayed for me at the miracle service and told me that the baby was healed. Brother Tracy also told us at the service not to worry that the baby was healed. Dan and I also felt confirmation that God had healed our baby boy.

The time came for our appointment with Dr. Moore at St. Johns. During the ultrasound, she began to explain that she could not find a cerebellum, but it may be that it is there; it was just abnormally small and may show up in a later ultrasound. She felt that he had a condition called Dandy Walker syndrome.

She also noticed that his skull was strawberry shaped due to pressure on his brain that could be caused from a neurotube defect called spina bifida. She immediately offered the option of abortion, and without hesitation we began to explain to her our strong faith in God. We let her know that we did not agree with abortion, and we wanted him to be born no matter what was wrong with him.

She then asked if we had any questions, and Dan asked her if she had ever seen a baby with these conditions be born completely normal. She responded, "No, not in the years that I have been in this field." He then let her know that we believed our baby could be born completely normal. We couldn't really think of any other questions at that time.

Dan was discouraged that we did not get the report we were expecting, but I let him know that I still felt he would be healed. It was just not God's time yet.

We had been trying to decide on what to name him, and I was reading about Abraham and Sarah and the miracle birth that they had with their son Isaac. We decided that it would be a testimony and a step of faith to name our son Isaac.

At our next appointment with Dr. Moore, she mentioned she thought she saw a cerebellum, but it was hard to see. She explained that there was pressure on Isaac's brain, but she was not sure why, that it could be caused from spina bifida, but they did not see any other signs of spina bifida. She called in another specialist, Dr. Ott, and he found a gap in Isaac's neurotube and spinal column. They concluded Isaac did have a form of spina bifida called meyelomenignocele. His neurotube and backbone where exposed, and they could not tell how big the hole was, but it was high enough in his back to be a big concern. She began to tell us what would happen once Isaac was born. I would have to have a scheduled C-section two weeks before my due date to insure that he was healthy enough to handle the surgery but early enough that the fluid on his brain would not start to cause too much damage. He would have to have an immediate surgery to close his back. He would never have movement past his hips because of where the defect was in his spine. He would not be able to control his bladder or his bowel movements on his own and may have to have surgeries for that down the road. He also had a condition called hydrocephalus or water on the brain due to pressure from the gap in his back.

Dan and I were glad to hear that this was all improved news and at least Isaac had a great chance of living now.

We continued to pray and received emails through my dad from people across the United States letting us know that they where praying for Isaac to be healed. We had such an assurance that God was going to heal Isaac that we began telling family, friends, church members, and people we worked with that we believed God was going to heal our son, and he would be born completely normal.

During the time leading up to his birth, we also had the World Network of Prayer, Prayer Summit at the church. This even built our faith more, and after the Sunday evening service, the Shekinah kids prayer group from the church prayed for Isaac and me.

A week later, late Monday night, January 24, I went into labor. My C-section was not scheduled for one more week, but Isaac was born by C-section on Tuesday, January 25, at 6:02 A.M.

As they were delivering him, Dan leaned over and let me know he did have a large hole in his back. I expected myself to be disappointed because we had no doubt that Isaac was already completely healed, but instead I continued to feel strength and faith knowing that was not God's plan. They began to work with him, covering his back, clearing his lungs and doing all the measurements. Even though he was three weeks early, he weighed 8 pounds, 2 ounces, and was 20 inches long. They took me to recovery, and Isaac to the NICU area. They had to put a breathing tube in because he had some fluid in his lungs and was having difficulty breathing on his own. They also started him on antibiotics immediately so his body could fight any infections. About three hours after he was born, I was able to see him for just a few minutes before they had to transport him to the NICU at Children's Hospital. Even though he had a lot of tubes and IV's he looked like a strong and healthy baby.

Dan went with Isaac, and I was taken to my room.

Once I was in the room, I just began to pray that we understood that God's plan was not our own and that He would still heal Isaac in His time.

Dan called shortly after to let me know that Isaac would have his first surgery at about 1:00, there would be two parts, a nerousurgery to repair his spine and a plastic surgery to put the muscles, tissue, and skin back together.

Dr. Smyth the neurosurgeon let Dan know this was his first time to operate on a meyelomenignocele this large, and it was only the ninth case he knew of this large. The surgeries would be about six hours combined. Dan and my dad let Dr. Smyth and Dr. Kane, the plastic surgeon, know that they would be praying that God would guide their hands during the surgeries.

Later that evening, Dan came back to see me and let me know that everything went really well. They were concerned that Isaac did not have enough skin to cover the hole, and they had to stretch it very tight since they do not graph at his age. But it was holding well as far as they could tell. Dan asked them what they would do if it did not hold and the surgeon's let him know they did not have a plan for that, just to pray.

He had some video of Isaac. This was the first time I had really got a good look at him. The incision on his back looked so big compared to his little body. It was very hard to watch. I felt very helpless not being able to be with him or see him, but every time I began to get upset, God continued to assure me that everything was in His hands.

The next day Dan said his back was looking a little better, it was not near as red. Dr. Smyth let us know that the pressure on Isaac's brain was increasing, and they where going to have to put in a shunt to relieve it. The next day on Thursday, Isaac had another surgery to have the shunt put in. Everything had went well, by now Dr. Smyth knew that we believed in prayer and let Dan know that if we were going to pray, pray that the shunt would not get infected. The risk of infection is one in three when they are newborns.

Over the next couple days, Dan would come back with good reports. He noticed Isaac move his right leg a little bit one time and he was opening his eyes and responding to Dan's voice, even holding his finger. Dan would also come back every evening with a list of babies in the NICU that needed prayer. He had came in contact with several of their family members while in the waiting room. We began to pray for them, and several of them got to go home before Isaac.

On that Saturday, I was finally able to go see him. His incision looked excellent. It was not even red any more. He was able to have his breathing tube taken out that morning. I met his physician, and he also let me know that they were going to try feeding him that evening and wanted me to be able to give him his first bottle. That evening I was able to hold him and feed him. He was so small and precious. I couldn't believe what a miracle he was already. He was able to have his feeding tube out the next day. They also let us know that he was having bowel movements on his own, but he was not emptying his bladder so he still had a catheter. The nurse also let me know that she had seen him move his right leg some, and he had turned his head from one side to another on his own.

The next few days went really well, and Isaac was able to be transferred to the "D" room, a room for more stable babies in the NICU the middle of that next week. There we met Melissa. She would be Isaac's nurse for the majority of the rest of his time in the NICU. That Sunday Isaac started to run a fever and was having trouble breathing on his own so he had to be put on oxygen. They put him on antibiotics to fight the infection and did tests to make sure it was nothing in his shunt. Dan and I prayed for him, like we did every time we would visit, and he did not run a fever anymore after Sunday. The tests came back, and it was not in the shunt, but the doctors let us know he was fighting an infection of some sort, but they were not sure what. They were also not completely sure why he was having an oxygen requirement again. His physician said they were not too concerned because he was acting like a completely healthy baby.

A couple of days later, his physician informed me that they were going to begin training me on how to catherize him on my own and said this would be something I would have to do three to four times a day since he was not able to empty his own bladder. Dan and I began praying specifically for this need and had others pray also. The next day the same physician had to explain the impossible to me. During the night, the nurse began to get empty catheters and noticed Isaac's diapers were full. He said he was not sure how this could be, but if it continued through the day, they would do a VCUG test to make sure he was actually going on his own. I was able to be with him later that afternoon for the test and watched on the x-ray as he emptied his own bladder. This was some of the most exciting news we had received so far!

Over the next week and a half, Isaac continued to improve. Every time I would visit, Melissa or his other nurses had nothing but good reports. He had physical therapy while he was in the NICU and was still moving his right leg every once in a while. He also began to have some of his stitches removed from his back and everything was healing great. Isaac did still have an oxygen requirement, but they said if we were comfortable and we completed some training, we could bring him home on the oxygen. We agreed and Isaac was able to come home on February 20.

He did really well and we were so excited to have him home. He started physical therapy in our home once a week and his movement in his right leg was getting a little better.

Dan and I were a little concerned about Isaac's medical expenses now that we were home, especially with all the home medical equipment we had, but we found out that we had reached a maximum amount while Isaac was in the NICU, and my insurance was covering everything after that point. This was a tremendous added blessing!

About a month later, Dan and I noticed Isaac was not being himself, he was fussy all the time and spitting up a lot. His head was also beginning to look a little swollen. We called Dr. Smyth, and I brought Isaac to Children's Hospital for a check up. They did a CT scan and discovered that Isaac's shunt was blocked. When I heard the news and found out we had only four hours to prepare for another surgery, I began to doubt God for the first time since Isaac was born. Immediately I caught myself and began to pray. I knew he promised to take care of Isaac, and once again I began to feel strength and faith that I will never be able to explain. Everything went well with the surgery, and Dr. Smyth let us know that they now had a new and improved shunt. It was full of antibiotics so there was not as high of a risk of infection. He also said that if everything went well, Isaac would only have to be in the hospital for two days.

We ended up having a roommate that had to have a shunt also. Her name was Ally. She was three, and this would be her first shunt. They lived three hours away. Her mom and her aunt were with her, and her mom was very upset. I was able to share Isaac's testimony with them and pray with them before she went into surgery. Isaac was able to come home on Thursday, just two days after the surgery, and Ally went home just one day after Isaac.

Friday the ladies' prayer group sent a prayer cloth to Isaac praying that he would be able to get off of the oxygen. I put the prayer cloth under Isaac's blanket that he slept on. That Sunday Isaac was doing very well, and we were able to take him off the oxygen. He has been off the oxygen every since. We give God all the glory!

He is doing excellent now, even beginning to sit up on his own. Three weeks ago on our first child, Cameron's, second birthday, Isaac began to move his right leg continuously as he sat on my lap. Since then he moves it very frequently and even moves his left every once in while now. His doctors still believe he will never be able to walk on his own, but we have seen God's hand on Isaac's life and know he will walk one day.

We are so thankful, not only for the miracles that God has done in Isaac's life, but also for all the doors that it has opened for us to reach out to others in need. It has not always been an easy road, but God has remained faithful and taught us that He has a master plan for Isaac. We have learned that He is always in control, and without a test, there can be no testimony for His glory!

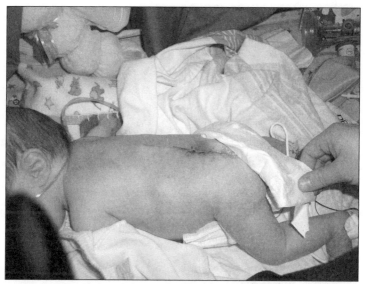

Two weeks old, after surgery on his back

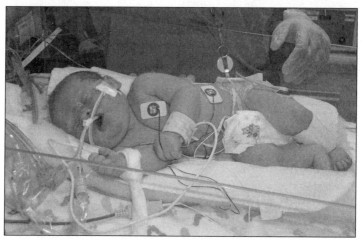

Three hours after birth, January 25, 2005

257

God Still Answers Prayer

Isaac's Dedication,
June 26, 2005

Second shunt surgery,
April 8, 2005

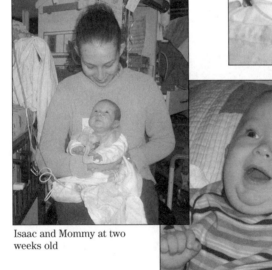

Isaac and Mommy at two
weeks old

Isaac laughing for one of the first times,
May 2005

45

Fear-Free Finances

by Claudette Walker

At the grocery store, many of us carefully scan the miniscule print to find the magic fat-free label on our food purchases. Although the fat-free food has yet to make us as "trim and slim" as we would like to be, I have discovered a fear-free approach to managing our finances that really works!

Actually, my parents taught me a fear-free financial lifestyle. When I was four years old, my father, Rev. R. P. Kloepper, was pastoring a home missions church in DuQuoin, Illinois. Dad had a degree in chemistry from Southern Illinois University and worked as a research chemist for United Electric. He had bought Mom her two-story dream house on a beautiful tree-lined street. They were financially secure with family living close by, and life was good. In 1955 when the superintendent of the Illinois District, Rev. M. J. Wolff, called Dad to consider becoming the superintendent of the Tupelo Children's Mansion, my mother had no interest in moving to Tupelo, Mississippi. The whole time we were visiting the Mansion, my mom kept her purse on her arm, ready to leave. However, for weeks afterward, as she swept the floors of her beautiful home, she would feel the pressure of four-year-old Faye's arms around her legs as Faye had hugged her and pleaded, "My momma is dead. Would you please come here and be my momma?"

After giving up their own plans and dreams, my parents sold the beautiful house. We moved into the boys' dormitory at the Mansion. The lifestyle change was different in every way but especially in the area of our finances. The Tupelo Children's Mansion was only two years old and still largely unknown in the United Pentecostal Church. Many overdue bills for the Mansion were stacked high on Mom's desk. Our family began to travel from state to state to raise money for the struggling orphanage. I vividly remember the night when my father came to my brother, Ray, and me after a conference service. "Kids, I really felt the Lord impress me to give fifty dollars in the offering. I have enough left so that we can either sleep in a motel or eat a meal and drive home all night. Which do you prefer?" My brother was quite clever and immediately voted to eat, knowing that he and I could sleep in the back seat while Dad drove all night. A wise father was purposefully planting in our hearts a seed of "Fear-Free Finances."

This experience was branded on my heart forever. I had learned for the first time that the best thing I can do with my money is to give it to bless God's kingdom! My parents lived before us a life of sacrificial giving. When he was seventy-one years old, Dad retired from pastoring in Superior, Wisconsin, and my parents moved back to Tupelo. Their income is now limited to Social Security checks. When they have extra needs, there are no funds available. One day in prayer, I was telling the Lord how financially desperate their situation was. "Lord, after a lifetime of sacrificial giving, Dad and Mom are elderly and are so financially insecure." The Lord interrupted my lament, "Claudette, there are few men on the earth as financially secure as your father." Wow! Did the Lord and I ever have different views of financial security! The Lord explained what He meant. "Because your parents have always given so abundantly of their finances to bless My work, now I am personally committed to meeting their needs." Immediately I thought of how some very rich people still feel so insecure and are always worrying if their carefully guarded stockpile of riches will be enough to meet their needs. Their feelings of security rise and fall with the stock market. I then realized how "secure" my father was in reality. After expressing a financial need to me, he would often say, "Sis, I can hardly wait to see how the Lord is going to miraculously supply this need."

One day they were getting ready to go to Sears to charge a washer and dryer since their very old ones were beyond repair. Before they could leave the house that morning, a truck pulled up to their door, delivering the Maytag washer and dryer that Mom had always wanted. Someone had heard of the need and owned a washer and dryer in storage that had only been used a few months. The gift was given anonymously, but its true source was a God who is very committed to meeting my parents' needs.

Almost as soon as my eighty-three-old dad's head lies on his pillow, he starts snoring. He thinks it is a sin to worry—an insult to a God who promised to care for our needs. He rests the blessed sleep of a child and feels very

261

secure in his Father's promised and certain care.

Jesus gave us instructions on how to trust Him with our needs and live the life of Fear-Free Finances. "Therefore take no thought, saying, What shall we eat? or, What shall we drink? or, Wherewithal shall we be clothed? (For all these things do the Gentiles seek:) for your heavenly Father knoweth that ye have need of all these things. But seek ye first the kingdom of God, and his righteousness; and all these things shall be added unto you. Take therefore no thought for the morrow: for the morrow shall take thought for the things of itself" (Matthew 6:31-34). My parents have lived their lives obeying Jesus' instructions in a practical manner, and they daily experience the joy of having Fear-Free Finances.

It is easy to tell our parents' stories, but the time comes to take our own steps of faith and watch the Lord provide for our own needs. About four years before our son, Jonathan, started college, we had readjusted our budget and had decided to put all the extra money each month into a college fund. It would not be enough to meet the need, but we were praying for scholarship money to supplement our savings. That fall Brother Jack Leaman preached our very first missions conference at our church in Cincinnati, Ohio. Brother Leaman spoke with such authority and anointing as he told so many stories of miraculous provision by God to those who had blessed worldwide missions with their finances. We had always given offerings beyond our tithing, but my husband, Marv, and I both felt the call of the Spirit to begin to give our budgeted college savings each month to Foreign Missions. We gladly turned in our Faith Promise form and began to claim the promise in Proverbs 13:22, "The wealth of the sinner is laid up for the just." We prayed, "Lord, we will gladly give our college savings monthly to Foreign Missions and trust You to send Jonathan to college."

Four years later, Jonathan was accepted into the University of Cincinnati's College of Engineering and was awarded a scholarship! God had answered our prayers and all was well until Jonathan told us how a panel of senior chemical engineering students talked to his class one day. They began to describe the wonderful job opportunities that would be offered to chemical engineers from this highly acclaimed engineering program. Salaries would be very substantial and even higher salaries would be offered to those choosing to obtain a master's degree. It all sounded very good to Jonathan until one student gave this warning: "I will tell you this, however. With your studies and co-op program which will begin your sophomore year, chemical engineering will consume your life for the next five years." Jonathan said the Spirit of the Lord moved on him so strongly, and God said to him, "It will not consume your life, Jonathan." After praying and consulting with us and school counselors, Jonathan felt he should change his major to communications, which would be of greater benefit to him in pursuing his call to full-time ministry. The only problem was that the scholarship was awarded only if he pursued the degree in chemical engineering. When we honor the Lord in our finances, He made a promise that we could "prove" Him. "Bring ye all the tithes into the storehouse, that there may be meat in mine house, and prove me now herewith, saith the LORD of hosts, if I will not open you the windows of heaven, and pour you out a blessing, that there shall not be room enough to receive it" (Malachi 3:10). And so we waited for God to open the windows of heaven.

The first miracle came in just a few weeks when a scholarship that had already been awarded to another was made available, and they gave it to Jonathan. We rejoiced together over God's first provision. In June 2002, as we sat and proudly watched Jonathan dressed in cap and gown as he came into the Shoemaker Center of the University of Cincinnati, I had meticulous records of $26,350 that had been given to Jonathan over the previous five years from seven different sources. Several sources were unsolicited and simply came to us through the open windows of heaven as God had promised. "Give, and it shall be given unto you; good measure, pressed down, and shaken together, and running over, shall men give into your bosom. For with the same measure that ye mete withal it shall be measured to you again" (Luke 6:38). The money we could have saved would not have been nearly enough to pay for Jonathan's college education, yet that same money blessed many missionaries and churches all over the world.

A beautiful example of a lady who learned this by a very traumatic experience is found in I Kings 17:1-16. God had miraculously provided for Elijah during a drought. Elijah drank water from the brook Cherith and ate bread and meat delivered twice a day by God-sent ravens. God could have allowed this to continue, but instead He allowed the brook to dry up. God then instructed Elijah to go to the city of Zarephath. In verse nine, the Lord said to Elijah, "I have commanded a widow woman there to sustain thee." When Elijah asked the widow for water and bread, we hear her desperation in verse twelve—"I have not a cake, but an handful of meal in a barrel, and a little oil in a cruse: and, behold, I am gathering two sticks, that I may go in and dress it for me and my son, that we may eat it, and die." It sounds like her biggest problem was that she and her son were soon to starve to death, but the prophet had been sent to her by God to deal with a bigger problem. The root of her problem we discover in verse thirteen when Elijah said to the widow, "FEAR NOT; go and do as thou hast said: but make me thereof a little cake first, and bring it unto me, and after make for thee and for thy son." The widow's greater problem was that she was afraid she would not have enough if she gave to the prophet first. She had a root of insufficiency in her spirit, and the Lord loved her so much that He wanted to remove it so she would no longer fear concerning her finances. Her loving Lord wanted to surgically remove that root of fear from her heart. The method He used was to ask her to give out of her desperate need to bless the man of God and in doing so to bless God's work. This widow chose to obey Elijah. We find the miraculous result of her obedience recorded in verse sixteen, "And the barrel of meal wasted not, neither did the cruse of oil fail, according to the word of the LORD, which he spake by Elijah." Just as this widow had the root of a fear of insufficiency removed from her heart through sacrificial giving, you and I can experience the same wonderful result if we will give to God's work out of our own desperate needs.

How very grateful I am to my parents who modeled before me how to have Fear-Free Finances! How very grateful I am to my husband who has consistently loved

God and His kingdom by consistently giving of our finances sacrificially! Above all, how very grateful I am to my Lord for always keeping His Word and providing miraculously for us during our thirty years of marriage! In a world where even rich men's hearts are fearful because of a very uncertain financial future, I am so thankful that I can lay my head on my heavenly Father's shoulder and rest the blessed rest of His children who are "secure" in a very insecure world. Thank You, Lord, for teaching me how to live with Fear-Free Finances!

Rev. R. P. and Betty Kloepper, Ray (9) & Claudette (4), 1955 at the Tupleo Children's Mansion

Rev. Marvin and Claudette Walker with son, Jonathan at graduation from
University of Cincinnati, June 2002

46

When Two Agree

by Mary Wallace

*I*n the spring of 1942, World War II was raging in Europe. J. O. Wallace had been drafted as a conscientious objector, true to the beliefs which his church had taught him. We had corresponded daily for over a year.

When J. O. asked me to marry him, I was thrilled but also apprehensive. What if he had to go overseas? What if he were badly wounded or killed? Our neighbor's son had already lost his life in a plane crash. Also Brother A. D. Gurley's son, Rentz, had been lost at sea. I wondered, "What would I do?" I was only eighteen years old, just graduating in May from Dyersburg High.

While reading my Bible one day, I found a scripture with a great promise—Matthew 18:19: "If two of you shall agree on earth as touching any thing that they shall ask, it shall be done for them of my Father which is in heaven." Jesus said that two could agree and God would answer.

"If you will agree with me that you won't be sent overseas, then I would love to go to California and be married,"

I wrote my sweetheart. He agreed with me. So we stood on God's promise in Matthew 18:19.

J. O. was based at Santa Barbara not too far from the coast which the Japanese had shelled. Since all furloughs were cancelled, J. O. could not come back to Tennessee for our wedding. My dear father agreed to go with me so I could marry my soldier. J. O. and I stood on God's promise in Matthew 18:19.

Because he had finished Draughn's Business College, the Army soon put J. O. to work in the office. Before we were married, his officer said, "Sargeant Wallace, they are using COs (conscientious objectors) now as officers in the Finance Department. You are officer material. You should apply to go to Officers Candidate School (OCS)."

We had only been married a week when his orders came. He was to report to Duke University for training. I rode the train with him to Tennessee, got off, and stayed with my parents while he was in training.

After just a few weeks at OCS, they issued arms for training. "I can't bear arms," J. O. explained. "I am classified as a conscientious objector."

So he was shipped out to Ogden Arsenal, a small base in Ogden, Utah. After a year, the War Department issued orders that they needed COs as officers. His captain again urged him to apply, and he was shipped to Camp Barkley in Abilene, Texas, to train.

The colonel there said, "I don't think a conscientious objector should be a commissioned officer." Later he informed J. O. that he was going to assign him to a unit in Minnesota scheduled to leave for overseas after completing their final training. "This unit needs a first sergeant."

When J. O. arrived in St. Paul, the officer in charge there said, "I have already filled that vacancy. You can stay with this unit or I can request reassignment."

"Give me a short furlough, and I'll find a place," J. O. responded. So we caught the train for Nashville, where he and his father had started a Pentecostal church in 1941 just before he was drafted. J. O. had supported not only the church he attended near the army base but also the West Nashville Pentecostal Church with his tithes. As a buck private, he only earned twenty-one dollars a month.

In Nashville the U.S. Army was building a new hospital. Thayer General Hospital on White Bridge Road was only a mile from his parents' home. When J. O. went out to the hospital, he met Captain Hirtle and told him, "I sure would like to be based here." Then he told the captain about his qualifications.

"Sit down at that typewriter and type out your request," the captain ordered.

In a few days, we were back home helping in the West Nashville Pentecostal Church and living off base with my husband's family.

The next summer, J. O. and his father, Rev. J. W. Wallace, held a revival in Goodlettsville, about thirty miles from West Nashville. Then they bought a church building on Depot Street. The commanding officer gave J. O. permission to live in Goodlettsville and pastor that mission church. He commuted to Thayer General Hospital daily. We started Goodlettsville Pentecostal Church with only two families: the Searcys and the Skimmyhorns—about fourteen people in all.

Meanwhile J. O.'s immediate superior officer, a warrant officer, had a drinking problem, so J. O. had almost full responsibility in the Army Personnel Department. I worked down the hall in the civilian personnel office. Thayer Hospital received one of the first boatloads of injured soldiers from Tunesia, North Africa. I wept as I typed up papers for paraplegics and other badly wounded young soldiers. Often we took some of them home with us for a home-cooked meal and a chance to go to church.

The warrant officer continued to hang out at a local bar. J. O. had to forge the officer's signature to important papers. Finally he complained to the commanding general. At first the general indicated that something would be done, but then he failed to follow through.

By this time, we were the proud parents of Jimmy Jr. and were pastoring our own church. But J. O. said, "I can't go on signing all these important papers." The only alternative was an overseas assignment. I was terribly upset. I wondered about Matthew 18:19.

They sent J. O. for his last overseas training and shipped him to the East coast to a port of embarcation. Brother W. T. Scott became the pastor of Goodlettsville Pentecostal Church.

Then came that wonderful news on May 9, 1945! V. E. Day! That dreadful world war was over in Europe! J. O. had served his country for four years and six months, so he had too many points to be assigned to overseas occupation duty!

Matthew 18:19 was a landmark answer to prayer in our marriage. Our Ebenezer! The U.S. Army just doesn't usually take orders from God.

Perhaps I was selfish in asking so much when friends and neighbors gave so much, but I was only an eighteen-year-old bride. I knew I needed my husband!

Since that time through sickness and health, for richer or poorer, in war and in peace, I know that God answers prayer!

Mary Wallace, high school

J. O. and Mary Wallace, wedding

47

Trouble in 2001

by Mary Wallace

I admit that I was concerned about the year 2000, the Millennium. I thought that perhaps we might have trouble with all those computers as predicted by many so-called experts. But we survived that year fine. It was the year 2001 that almost did us in.

My daughter said I began to complain of stomach distress around Thanksgiving of 2000. But by Christmas I could not even enjoy a delicious dinner at my son's house. I tried Pepcid, then someone suggested Zantac. Nothing seemed to give relief.

Sometime before that, J. O.'s doctor had discovered trouble with his prostate gland, but he refused any further talk about treatment until after the holidays. Then we got the dreaded diagnosis: prostate cancer. Radiation treatments must begin right away. This entailed a twenty-mile trip across town to St. Thomas Cancer Clinic for radiation each day.

At the same time, I suffered pain after eating each meal. After a few weeks, my daughter Margie said, "Mom, it sounds like gallbladder trouble to me." Tests revealed that I did have two gallstones, so I had surgery for that, made a quick recovery, and soon was again taking J. O. to the cancer clinic five days a week.

But my stomach distress did not clear up, and I began to lose weight. I just could not eat without pain. "But J. O. has cancer," I thought. "I don't have time to be sick. Surely some sort of medication will help." But nothing stopped the pain after each meal.

Finally, about the last of June, my daughter-in-law, Carla, said, "Memaw, you are sick! I'm going to take you to the doctor." So she did and spoke very frankly to my internist, who immediately ordered tests.

When I called to hear the results of the tests, he said, "Call your surgeon, Dr. Mulherin, immediately." When I went to the surgeon, he told me, "Your stomach has gone up through your diaphragm and has wrapped around your esophagus. When the blood supply is cut off from the stomach, it dies." Then he pointed his finger at me and said, "Then you die!"

"All right, when do we operate?" I asked.

"I already have two surgeries in the morning," he answered.

"How about tomorrow afternoon?" I knew that my daughter, Rosemary, who lived in Mississippi, could be here by then. Rose is a nurse, and I definitely wanted her with me.

So I had the surgery the very next day. It was horrendous! I was so sick I could hardly move, with a long incision. After seven days in the hospital, I came home.

On Sunday morning, I had eased out to the front porch to sit in the morning sun. Suddenly I heard my son

Jeff call, "Mom, Dad has fallen out of bed!"

I hurried to J. O.'s bedroom and found him on the floor. "Call an ambulance," I insisted. "He may have broken a hip or his back!"

We called our second son, Jack, who with his nurse wife, Joanne, met J. O. at the emergency room. Jeff stayed home with me.

X-rays revealed nothing broken. When Jack called Rosemary, who had just gotten back home in Mississippi, she inquired, "Why did he fall? Is he dizzy? Tell them to do a CAT scan."

The CAT scan revealed a tumor on the front portion of the brain. Meanwhile Jeff and I sat on the porch in the sunshine trying not to worry, wondering why they were so long. But when I would call Jack, he would only say, "They are trying to find out what's wrong, Mom. We'll call when we know something." They admitted J. O. to the hospital and began to try to shrink the tumor some and relieve a little of the swelling.

We all had noticed a difference in my husband for the last several months. He had lost a lot of strength and slept a lot, didn't talk much. But we thought it was the radiation treatments and the dread of cancer.

The brain surgeon sent him home for a few days to try to reduce the swelling. Then he scheduled the surgery. Meanwhile, the saints in the Nashville churches and friends in St. Louis and other places were praying for us, sending food, and visiting. Thank God, when Dr. Standard operated, he was able to remove the tumor. It was not entwined nor malignant although the doctor said it was a fast-growing sort of tumor.

Meanwhile, I was recovering slowly with the help of

my children and home health care. We had to have help around the clock for J. O. When I called the ministers here in Nashville, they kindly helped with the 7:00 A.M. to 3:00 P.M. shift. My sons came after work and stayed until 11:00; then we hired help for the late night shift. The nurses said we must have someone with him lest he fall and injure his head surgery. After about ten days in the hospital, J. O. came home to recover with the help of others.

Thank God for His continuing care and comfort. With His help and the prayers and assistance of His people, we survived those most serious problems. He is so faithful!

48

Back Problems

by Mary Wallace

*I*n December 1997, I took the flu, then had Christmas houseguests plus hosted a dinner party for thirty visitors. On Tuesday after the holiday rush, I tried to get back to routine but could not get into the bath. My husband helped me back to bed. "Just let me rest a day or so," I said. But days passed, and I found I could hardly walk across the room.

When I saw my doctor, he said, "Bursitis," and gave me a shot of cortisone along with an anti-inflammatory drug and strong painkillers. This helped a little but walking was still very difficult even on a walker.

A copy of the MRI report January 19 showed lumbar spondylosis and degenerative disc change at multiple levels, severe acquired stenosis, and other scary sounding findings. Another doctor said, "Your back has been broken at some time!" There was nothing more that they could do, so they sent me to a neurosurgeon.

"Mrs. Wallace, I see you are on a quad cane, so aren't you improving some? I can operate if you insist, but you will not be like new. It may relieve a little of the pain," the neurosurgeon said.

"Well, I am sure not insisting on surgery," I answered. "I think I can handle the pain."

"Keep your job at the bookstore. Get up and get out of the house every day," the doctor prescribed.

So I continued to walk using the quad cane, taking Daypro and Darvocet painkillers several times a day. I found myself becoming very depressed.

"That Darvocet can cause depression along with other side effects," a friend who was also a physician warned me. So I stopped taking it except every two or three nights when I could not sleep because of the pain.

When I wrote my Christmas cards, I said, "1998 has been a very different year, but I am still able to walk with a cane and I am working every day."

On December 10, Pastor Lillian G. Hedges, an old friend who pastors United Pentecostal Church of South Pittsburg, Tennessee, wrote as follows:

My dear Brother and Sister Wallace,
Praise the Lord!
I can certainly relate to 1998 being different! As you probably heard, I had a heart attack May 24 at the South Pittsburg church. I had just left the radio station at 7:40 A.M. [Sister Hedges has preached on the radio for several years.] The attack was terrible! I was dying in the church, but I was certainly praying. I began to rebuke Satan and then I rebuked death in Jesus' name! I began to get some relief. By ten o'clock when it was time for church, I went ahead and had Sunday school and church service. By 11:45 I was leaving. I told one lady, "I'm

going home and going to the emergency room."

She said, "You're not—get in the car—I'm taking you to the hospital" (about five blocks from the church).

After telling me, I'd had a heart attack—they put me in ICU, then on Wednesday sent me by ambulance to Park Ridge Hospital in Chattanooga. On Friday I had open-heart surgery with four bypasses! I'm going strong—as usual! Doing pretty well. Thanks to Jesus!

I've seen many miracles of healings, even the dead raised. I prayed for a lady in the church here who died in the recovery room in North Jackson South Hospital. I walked in and anointed her forehead and began saying, "Jesus, Jesus," for three or four minutes, and she came back to life. Dr. Elmore was amazed, and he told everybody that no one could make him doubt "God could do a miracle."

Sister Wallace, God has laid on my heart to anoint a handkerchief and pray for you. God is still just the same! I'm just Lillian, but my God is "special." As we agree, we bind and rebuke Satan together in Jesus' name!

This handkerchief is new. I just took it out of the box. I bought it in the Philippines in 1985 while there with you (for the UPC World Conference)! Maybe this is why I've never used it.

I am a miracle. I rebuked death and the devil in Jesus' name! The doctor told me that he was amazed at me. He agreed it was the Lord!

God bless you both with a wonderful holiday season!

We love you.

Sister Hedges

Since I received that wonderful letter from a praying woman, I take very little medication, usually just one

Aleve a day. My left leg is still numb, and I usually have some low-level pain but ordinarily nothing that prevents a good night's sleep. I'm still working five days a week in the bookstore and writing books at night. Thank God for Sister Hedges' healing and for her ministry to me. She has been a faithful prayer warrior and pastor in Tennessee for many years. (Read her great story in *Pioneer Pentecostal Women, Volume III*.)

49

From Suffering to Glory

by Barbara Washburn

*I*n June of 1997, Brother Darful Thomason was diagnosed with mystastic thyroid carsonoma cancer. Surgery was performed and treatment was given. Against his wishes, he found himself thrust into a new lifestyle to which he was not accustomed. No one is ever ready for the agony of a terminal illness. After being referred to an oncologist for follow up, he was in and out of the hospital several times for treatment and surgery.

The cancer began to spread and grow until the fall of 2001. He was given a PET scan to locate any cancer cells in the body. A solution of glucose and radioactive iodine was given intravenously which would cause the cancer cells to glow. He lay strapped to a cot with his arms above his head for four hours until the procedure was complete. The results were not good. Cancer cells were spotted in various parts of his body . . . saliva glands, left shoulder, both lungs, stomach, bladder, and urinary track. Naturally, the diagnosis was very disturbing.

Darful was being treated by an oncologist at Baptist

Hospital in Nashville. After consulting other doctors across the country, it was determined that he would have a choice of Anderson Hospital in Houston, Texas, or Vanderbilt Hospital in Nashville, Tennessee, for surgery. He chose Vanderbilt and the oncologist was Dr. James Netterville.

Before Darful went to surgery in February 2002, Brother Ron Becton, his pastor, and Brother Tony Larkins, his son-in-law (also a pastor), were there to pray before he was taken to the operating room. Dr. Netterville, who is excited about Pentecostal worship, told Brother Becton and Brother Larkins, "I believe in divine healing, and God's taking care of us. It is not unusual for me to stop during a surgery and ask God to direct my hands to do what needs to be done."

It is a good feeling to know that you are in the care of someone who believes in prayer, healing, and the direction of God. Darful's family was always with him to pray and help make decisions. His pastor, assistant pastor, and other couples from church were there to pray as well. In addition to that, there was a prayer meeting going on at church. During the seven and a half-hour surgery, Dr. Netterville removed cancer from his esophagus, the left shoulder and a cancerous tumor in his windpipe. They had to cut his windpipe in two and sew it back together. In so doing, they damaged his vocal cords, and it was hard for him to breathe.

Three days after that surgery, he had to have emergency surgery. During the first surgery, they had removed so much of his esophagus that it was very thin and it had ruptured, thus creating more problems. His body began to swell, his temperature rose and he became incoherent.

In the second surgery, they went into the left shoulder and took a muscle up to his esophagus so they could build a cushion. When they did that, the healing process began. He was fed by a tube, which is very painful, but God was with him. It was a month before he could go home.

During his convalescence, Darful was going through his wife's study Bible one day and found something she had written. It read: "Cancer is limited and it cannot cripple love. It cannot shadow hope. It cannot corrode faith. It cannot destroy peace. It cannot kill friendship. It cannot suppress memories. It cannot silence courage. It cannot invade the soul. It cannot steal eternal life. It cannot conquer the spirit." It was so encouraging to him to read what she had written. Darful and Mary Ann had already claimed a scripture: "For I reckon that the sufferings of this present time are not worthy to be compared with the glory which shall be revealed in us" (Romans 8:18). They had not told anyone in their family that they had claimed that scripture, but Erin, their granddaughter, was in Bible quizzing. They were studying the Book of Romans, and Erin told her mother that this scripture was for her grandfather. What a confirmation!

In times of extended illness, it is so easy to become discouraged and depressed. God knows what you are going through, and He has a way of sending someone to minister to you when you need help. It happened three times for Darful Thomason. The first time because he couldn't breathe or swallow and he felt like he was choking to death. There was no way he could rest. About 3 A.M. a nurse came in and said, "Mr. Thomason, you're not resting."

"I know," he replied.

"I will have to get you some medicine because you need to rest," she insisted.

"Please don't give me any medicine," he begged. "I don't want to go to sleep. I want to stay awake."

"I don't know about that," she said.

"Please don't get me any medicine. I don't want to go to sleep," he begged again.

Darful was afraid that if he shut his eyes, he would never see again. He was having a hard time breathing as it was, and if he went to sleep, he might not be able to breathe at all. The nurse didn't give him any medicine, and he stayed awake all night. After he went home and felt better, he went to church one Sunday morning and gave his testimony in Sunday school class. After class, Brother John Kennedy told him that one morning while Darful was in the hospital, he woke up at 3 A.M. with Darful on his mind. He got out of bed and prayed for him. No doubt, that prayer made a big difference for Darful that morning. When God speaks to you about someone, it is for a reason. Don't ever ignore it or shrug it off!

The second time was on a Wednesday, Darful was home, and he had been having a bad day, both mentally and physically. About 9:00 that night, he was sitting in a recliner next to his bed. His wife was in another chair in the same room. They heard a car speeding up the driveway. They wondered who in the world could be speeding up their driveway that time of night. Soon, the doorbell rang and they went to the door. It was Sister Jane Ginn. She said, "I can't stay, but we had a prayer march at church tonight. We prayed for you and others who needed a touch from the Lord."

She handed him a prayer cloth and left. They went back into the bedroom. He sat down in the recliner, and they put the cloth on his throat. Mary Ann got down on her knees and they prayed. God performed a miracle that night and Darful felt so much better.

The third time was on a Monday morning. Again, he was feeling bad and depressed. About 11:30, soothing warmth came over his body that brought relief and tranquility. Later, he found out that some ladies were having a prayer meeting at church that morning. He knows they prayed for him because God became real to him that day.

Darful had one more surgery in December 2002. Today he is cancer free, but he still has to have regular check-ups. His life is another wonderful testimony to the love and mercy that Jesus bestows on those who commit their lives to Him.

Barbara Washburn

50

Is That You, Lord?

by Barbara Washburn

It was Sunday morning and meeting time at the Clark Hill church in Olive Hill, Kentucky. Myrt Wilson got up at 4 A.M. and began to prepare breakfast for her husband, Bob, and her son, Herb. For some reason, she started thinking about Addie Sammons. Mrs. Sammons was her neighbor, who lived up the road about a quarter of a mile. Mrs. Sammons had heart dropsy and her legs were badly swollen. One time they burst open, and she had to go to the hospital. Her husband, Will, had to do all the housework and take care of her.

Myrt finished cooking breakfast and they ate. All the time, she was still thinking about Mrs. Sammons. She cleared the table and went to work on her dinner. Company would be coming home with her from church, so she cooked a better-than-average meal. She had made desserts the night before. Now she boiled a hen for dumplings. The beans were already cooking. All the time she was cooking, she couldn't get Mrs. Sammons off her mind. Was something wrong, or was it just a thought?

When her dinner was finished, Myrt hurried to the bathroom to get ready to go to church. Bob was the head deacon. It was his job to bring the pans and towels for the footwashing. Myrt made the unleavened bread, and Bob bought grape juice for communion.

They arrived at church, set up the communion table, and greeted people as they came in. Myrt would talk to someone for a few minutes, then her mind would drift back to Mrs. Sammons. Soon the song service began. Myrt sang with the rest of the congregation, but her mind was on Mrs. Sammons. During the preaching, she tried to concentrate, but all she could think about was Mrs. Sammons. By this time, Myrt was sure there must be a problem. She was anxious for the service to end so she could go see what was wrong. Preaching, communion, and footwashing seemed to take forever.

When the service finally ended, Bob and Myrt looked for people who had driven long distances to come to church that day. "Go home with us for dinner," they invited. When she got home, Myrt quickly set dinner on the table, then told her company to help themselves. "I need to go see about my neighbor."

Myrt and Bob knocked on the door expecting Will to answer, but he didn't. They thought they heard Addie tell them, "Come on in." When they went inside, they found that Will had been passed out all morning and was still in the bed. Addie hadn't eaten anything or taken her medicine. The Sammons didn't have a phone, so all Addie could do was pray for someone to come to help her. She had tried to call Will, but he didn't answer.

Myrt went back to her house and prepared the Sammonses a plate while explaining to her company about the Sammons' problem. She and Bob took the food to her neighbors. Then Myrt stayed with Addie and Will while Bob went to town to get the doctor. The doctor was able to revive Will. When they saw that he was going to be all right, they left.

All of Myrt's company agreed that it was a good thing that she had gone to see about Addie. They treated her like a hero. Although her response had been delayed because of chores and not really being sure that it was the Lord speaking to her, Myrt had answered the call. How much better would it have been if she had answered the call early that morning when the Lord had first spoken to her?

Sometimes we're not sure if it is the Lord talking to us, or if we just imagined it. As you spend time with the Lord, you learn to recognize His voice. Being submissive and obedient will sharpen your sensitivity to the Holy Ghost. Above all we must respond with faith, for we know God does answer prayer!

Will and Addie Sammons, 1959

Bob and Myrt Wilson, 1963

51

A Simple Prayer

by Barbara Washburn

obby Williams and his family were not accustomed to attending church. However, Bobby's aunt, Fay Martin, attended the Old Hope Church of Christ in Boston, Tennessee. Most of the members were middle-aged or elderly people. The pastor encouraged the congregation, "Find some young people and invite them to church."

In response to this appeal, Fay asked Bobby to let his two sons, Robert and Steven, go to church with her. They went a few Sundays and liked it so well that they talked their mother, Betty, into going with them.

The boys kept asking their dad to go, but he always had some excuse. After a few weeks of being coaxed and bribed, Bobby finally promised the boys that he would go the next Sunday.

That Saturday Bobby had to repair the brakes on his car. He started early so he could finish in time to do some other chores. First, he had to get the old brakes off. He started taking the bolts off, but there was one that had been in place so long that it was rusted. It would not budge. He tried using other wrenches and different techniques. He put rust remover on it and beat and banged on it. Nothing worked. By afternoon, he was really aggravated.

While he was struggling with that bolt, his older son, Robert, came out and asked, "Dad, are you going to church with us in the morning?"

In his frustration, Bobby yelled, "How do you think I can go to church in the morning when I can't get this car fixed?"

Disappointed, Robert went back into the house. Bobby started feeling guilty because he had talked so roughly to his son. He laid his tools down, got on his feet, and went inside. He got a drink of water and sat down at the table. He apologized to Robert and said, "If I can get that car fixed this evening, I'll go to church in the morning."

Bobby finished his water and went back to the car, picked up his wrench, and placed it over the bolt. He prayed, "Lord, if you will help me get this car fixed, I'll go to church in the morning." He prepared to turn the bolt with all his might. To his amazement, the bolt came off as if it were barely in place. By dark, the brakes were repaired. The next morning Bobby kept his promise and went to church. Then he started attending regularly.

Today Bobby and his family are faithful members of the church. Bobby is the song leader and participates in other activities as well. He has a church home and the hope of eternal salvation. He has strong faith and is blessed physically and spiritually. It all started with a simple prayer.

52

At Death's Door

by Barbara Washburn

*I*n August 2000, Clarence (Butch) Helton entered Centennial Medical Center in Nashville, Tennessee, for back surgery. For thirty years, Butch had taken pain pills for temporary relief. Now there was hope that he would have a permanent healing. The surgery went well. In a few days, he went home.

Two or three weeks later, he began to get sick. He got worse before he or his wife, Evelene (a nurse), realized what had happened. In severe pain, he was rushed back to the hospital. An MRI revealed a staph infection that was out of control. Immediately they started giving him antibiotics by IV. He remained on the medication for six weeks. As long as he was on the medication, he was fine. However, he could not stay on it any longer because too much of it would destroy his vital organs.

After a few days when the medicine wore off, he was sick again. Tremendous pain gripped his body and sapped his energy. For the second time, he was rushed to the hospital. They did another MRI, which revealed that the infection was back. This time they decided that since the antibiotics were not helping, they would surgically clean all the infection off his spine. In a few days, Butch was released but was told to stay on the antibiotics. At times the pain was so severe that he could not move without literally screaming. Morphine and other strong medicines gave only a small amount of temporary relief. It was a terrible ordeal at the time, but in a few weeks, he was better. Seeing a significant improvement in his condition, the doctor took him off the antibiotics.

As before, in just a few days, Butch was sick again and the pain in his back was almost unbearable. Soon he was back to the old familiar routine—hospital, MRI, more infection, more antibiotics.

He went to church on a Sunday night in late November or early December. He was sick but not as sick as he had been. It was a great service. During the altar call, Brother Ron Becton, his pastor, went back to the pew where Butch was sitting and took him to the altar. They prayed for almost an hour, and Brother Becton proclaimed that it was the beginning of a slow healing process in Butch's body. That encouraged Butch and Evelene.

A few weeks later, on Christmas Eve, Butch was rushed to the hospital again. They took him into surgery immediately and surgically removed the infection as they had done before. After surgery, they put him in a room and back on antibiotics.

In a few days, Butch went home, but he just lay around the house in such pain and agony that he couldn't get off the couch or out of bed without screaming. Evelene was trying to work, but she was very worried about him.

While he was in one hospital, she was working in another. The doctors had done all they knew to do and nothing was working. Hallucinating and delirious from pain and medication, Butch tried to get out of the bed by himself and fell in the hospital floor.

Through it all, God had His hand on Butch Helton. There was not a time from August until the following May that he was ever permitted to know how close he came to death. Butch found out later that on that Christmas Eve, the doctor was ready to order a casket for him because of the seriousness of his condition. But it never entered Butch and Evelene's minds that he might die. The church prayed and the mighty hand of God was there to sustain them and bring them hope. Having been at death's door more than once, Butch can certainly testify to the power of prayer.

In February it seemed as if God decided that Butch had suffered enough. He finally showed the doctors a new drug called Zyvox. The drugstores didn't have it because the cost was four thousand dollars for a thirty-day supply and not many people could afford it. After taking Zyvox three months, Butch was finally healed of the deadly infection.

As he recalls his time of illness, Butch can testify that God is a miracle worker who spared his life more than once. Not only is he grateful for healing, but he has a deep appreciation for a church family that supported him with cards, prayers, and phone calls. He admits that he used to halfheartedly pray for people who were sick or had a problem, like, "Lord, help them if You can." Now he remembers what a blessing others were to him. He purposed in his heart that when someone needed encouragement, he would gladly give it. When they are sick, he will pray fervently. If they need a helping hand, he will lend it. Most of all he will never again take the blessings of God's mercy and faithfulness for granted.

Clarence (Butch) Helton by the limousine he drove, 1995.

Clarence (Butch) Helton, 2002.

53

No Doubt About It

by Barbara Washburn

It was a December Sunday morning in 2001. Loretta Taylor and her grandson, Travis, were on their way to church. As they got close to Nashville, Travis said, "Grandma, stop at Toys "R" Us. I want to show you something else I want for Christmas."

Inside the store, Loretta began to feel sick and started shaking uncontrollably. "Am I taking the flu?" she wondered. She took Travis on to church but told one of the ushers that she was going home. "I'm sick. Be sure to find Travis a ride home with some of the family."

"Do you want someone to take you home?" the usher asked.

"No, I think I can make it," she answered. Later she admitted that as sick as she was, that was a foolish mistake.

When Loretta got home, she told her husband, Horace, "I'm going to bed. I'm sick. Don't let anyone in because I think I may have a bad case of the flu."

The next morning she was not better, but worse.

Since she was so sick, she was hardly aware of what was going on, but she can recall just two things about going into the hospital. Kim Tyler, her nephew's wife (a nurse), came in and asked, "What are you doing on this floor?"

Loretta doesn't remember her answer, but she does remember the extremely painful bone marrow biopsy. In her confusion, she could not understand why she was going through all of this for the flu. Before she left the hospital, the doctor made her an appointment to see an oncologist the next week. Why would he send her to an oncologist for the flu? Loretta could not figure it out.

She kept the appointment, but she felt strange surrounded by cancer patients. After an examination and blood tests, the doctor said, "You have borderline leukemia." He started her on some strong medicine. "Take this until you come back to see me." Since Loretta was not at all satisfied with that diagnosis, she went to another oncologist and asked, "Please tell me what is wrong with me."

After another examination and more blood tests, that doctor also said, "You have borderline leukemia. You are a very sick lady."

On a Sunday night in February, Loretta went to church to hear Brother Ethan Hagan preach. He asked for anyone who needed a miracle to stand and for others to gather around that person and pray. Loretta never even noticed who was praying for her. Instead of thinking of herself, she began to pray for Miles Pope, a little boy who had undergone surgery for a growth on his spine. As people prayed for Loretta, she felt as if all her blood ran out her feet and came back up again as hot as it could be. She told Brother Hagan, "I believe God has healed me tonight."

"Claim it!" Brother Hagan insisted.

She kept her appointment with the first cancer doctor. He said, "Loretta, I want you to start taking a shot every day. It would be a lot better if someone in your family could do it rather than for you to have to come to the clinic every day. That could be very expensive."

He made out a schedule whereby she would take a shot a day for several weeks. Then she would take two shots a week for a while, still later one shot a month. After he finished making the schedule, the doctor sent her to have blood work done. About thirty minutes later, he came back and asked, "What have you been doing?"

"Whatever you said for me to do," she replied.

"You can forget those shots every day. Your blood is perfect! But what have you done?"

"It's not anything that anyone else has done," she answered. "I believe God has healed me."

The doctor did not want to talk about that. After Loretta got the report from the oncologist, she had to return to her primary care doctor. With a look of surprise, that doctor exclaimed, "Loretta, what has happened?"

"Dr. Lacey, God has healed me," Loretta answered.

"It had to be," Dr. Lacey admitted. "There's not a medicine in the world that could have made your blood as good as it is today. You are a walking miracle!"